The Psychology of Financial Wellbeing

Grounded in Positive Economic Psychology theory and research, *The Psychology of Financial Wellbeing: An Introduction* offers a comprehensive introduction to the key concepts, models and theories that inform financial wellbeing.

Financial wellbeing is a state of being where a person or a household can meet their financial obligations, feel secure about their financial future and are able to make choices that allow them to fulfil their needs and enjoy life. This book clarifies the foundational concepts underpinning financial wellbeing, defines the concept and outlines its indicators and core components. It also synthesises the research evidence on the factors that foster financial wellbeing and presents a novel model that offers a comprehensive blueprint for pursuing financial wellbeing.

Written in a clear, balanced and accessible style, this textbook is an essential read for anyone looking to achieve financial prosperity, resilience and wellbeing. It will interest students across Economics, Business, Clinical Psychology, Social Psychology, Positive Psychology, Economic and Consumer Psychology, Education, Social Work, Coaching and Financial Planning, as well as professionals looking to understand how financial wellbeing can be applied in their own work.

Rona Hart is an Associate Professor in Applied Positive Psychology at the School of Psychology, University of Sussex, UK. She is a lecturer, researcher, practitioner and author specialising in Positive Psychology and Economic Psychology. Recently, she has launched a pioneering interdisciplinary field, Positive Economic Psychology, which integrates these two domains. Her textbook *Positive Psychology: The Basics* (Routledge) is widely adopted in higher education and has been translated into multiple languages. Rona is also a longstanding member of the International Positive Psychology Association (IPPA) and holds several leadership roles. Rona is also a Co-editor of the *International Journal of Wellbeing* and served as guest editor for several special issues.

The Psychology of Financial Wellbeing

An Introduction

Rona Hart

Routledge
Taylor & Francis Group
LONDON AND NEW YORK

Designed cover image: Getty Images

First published 2027
by Routledge
4 Park Square, Milton Park, Abingdon, Oxon OX14 4RN

and by Routledge
605 Third Avenue, New York, NY 10158

Routledge is an imprint of the Taylor & Francis Group, an informa business

British Library Cataloguing-in-Publication Data
A catalogue record for this book is available from the British Library

ISBN: 9781032541075 (hbk)
ISBN: 9781032541068 (pbk)
ISBN: 9781003415176 (ebk)

DOI: 10.4324/9781003415176

Typeset in Sabon
by Deanta Global Publishing Services, Chennai, India

Contents

List of Illustrations

1 Introduction

In the complex tapestry of human life, money stands out as a critical theme. However, discussions about it often swing between the cold calculations of income, savings, debt and interest rates, and the emotional narratives of needs, desires, happiness, stress, success and failure. This book seeks to unify these perspectives and delve into the psychology of financial wellbeing.

Historically, the concept of financial wellbeing has been predominantly framed within the discipline of Economics and the practice of Financial Planning. While many equate financial wellbeing purely with the numbers on their bank statements or the size of their investment portfolios, the true nature of financial wellbeing is much more complex. At its core, financial wellbeing encompasses not only our monetary assets, but also our psychology: our attitudes, beliefs and emotions, and the ways in which these shape our financial decisions, behaviours and actions, and influence our economic outcomes.

This book offers an introduction to the scholarly work that has conceptualised, analysed and discerned the factors that can determine, maintain or enhance a state of optimal financial wellbeing in individuals and households. In exploring these topics, it takes an interdisciplinary approach that combines insights from Economic Psychology and Positive Psychology to present a comprehensive understanding of financial wellbeing. The book aspires to help individuals and organisations understand and develop psychological and economic mechanisms that can promote financial prosperity, resilience, wellbeing and security.

The book takes readers on a journey that commences with an overview that sets the stage for the scientific exploration of financial wellbeing. The book opens by exploring Positive Economic Psychology, the bedrock of financial wellbeing, and this is followed by examining money matters and wellbeing – the two key components brought together in the concept of financial wellbeing. The following chapter explores the contemporary conceptualisations of financial wellbeing. The subsequent chapter reviews key models that explore the determinants of financial wellbeing, and this is followed by a novel applied model which offers readers a practical roadmap to financial wellbeing. The final chapter investigates the outcomes of financial wellbeing, addressing psychological wellbeing, physical health, work and relationships.

DOI: 10.4324/9781003415176-1

Chapter 2: Positive Economic Psychology

This introductory chapter delves into the emerging interdisciplinary field of Positive Economic Psychology, establishing the philosophical groundwork for the research and application of financial wellbeing. The chapter provides an overview of its two contributing disciplines – Positive Psychology and Economic Psychology, and elucidates the mission, principles and scope of the new field. The chapter concludes with an evaluation of the field's future prospects.

Chapter 3: Money Matters

This chapter lays the foundation for exploring financial wellbeing by examining the complex nature of money: its diverse forms, functions and significance within economic systems. It further details the key methodologies employed in contemporary research for measuring financial resources, encompassing micro and macro, objective, subjective, absolute and relative measures.

Chapter 4: Wellbeing and Happiness

Financial wellbeing is a subset of overall wellbeing, while financial satisfaction is considered a specific aspect of global happiness. To better understand financial wellbeing, this chapter delves into the complex nature of the broader concepts of wellbeing and happiness. The chapter defines wellbeing and happiness, elucidates the connection between these concepts, explores their various components and sub-domains and discusses the different approaches to measuring these constructs.

Chapter 5: Financial Wellbeing

This chapter delves into the book's central theme: financial wellbeing. It begins by defining financial wellbeing, dissecting its key components and examining its measurement tools. The chapter then explores several intersecting concepts, such as financial satisfaction, stress, resilience and security, clarifying both the connections and differences between these concepts.

Chapter 6: Models of Financial Wellbeing

This chapter reviews several contemporary scholarly models that summarise and delineate the determinants of financial wellbeing and its outcomes. The chapter also critiques the existing literature, highlighting gaps and opportunities for further research.

Chapter 7: A Novel Model of Financial Wellbeing

A novel model of financial wellbeing is the focal point of this chapter. Drawing on principles of Positive Economic Psychology, this applied model is intended to offer a comprehensive blueprint for pursuing financial wellbeing. Structured as a hierarchy, the model includes six tiers: financial dispositions and outlooks, financial capabilities, planning and decision-making, social context, financial behaviours and accomplishments. The chapter also provides evidence to support the inclusion of each factor in the model.

Chapter 8: The Downstream Effects of Financial Wellbeing

This chapter outlines how financial wellbeing (and its absence) spills over into multiple life domains. It summarises evidence linking financial wellbeing to health, psychological factors, relationships, work and financial activity. It also considers how these outcomes can become self-reinforcing, creating cycles that deepen financial vulnerability over time.

The aim of this book is simple yet ambitious: to provide a comprehensive resource that not only enlightens but also empowers. Whether you're a professional in the field, researcher, lecturer, student or curious reader seeking to improve your relationship with money, this book aims to offer you valuable insights and practical tools to enhance your financial wellbeing. The pages ahead explore numbers, accounts, or investments, as well as the fabric of our emotions, perceptions and motivations as they intertwine with our financial choices. It therefore presents a journey of introspection alongside strategy, leading us towards a deeper understanding of what it truly means to achieve and maintain financial wellbeing.

2 Positive Economic Psychology

These are defining times for Positive Economic Psychology! Launched in 2025 as a novel interdisciplinary field that integrates Positive Psychology and Economic Psychology (Hart & Hart, 2025), it is currently undergoing a phase of rapid expansion and exploration, and is attracting considerable interest from the scientific community, practitioners across diverse fields and the general public.

This introductory chapter maps the intellectual terrain of this emerging field, which forms the groundwork for the psychological conception of financial wellbeing. The chapter opens with an overview of its two foundational disciplines, Positive Psychology and Economic Psychology. Subsequently, the chapter delves into the background that led to the emergence of Positive Economic Psychology, examining its core mission, remit and guiding principles. The chapter concludes by evaluating the prospective path of the discipline and identifying potential obstacles it might encounter.

POSITIVE PSYCHOLOGY

Positive Psychology is a branch of Psychology that was launched as a scientific and applied field in 1998 (Seligman & Csikszentmihalyi, 2000). While at the time of inception there were significant misconceptions about its remit, and it was dubbed as "happiology", today it is recognised as "the science and practice of improving wellbeing" (Lomas et al., 2014, p. ix), or more broadly as "the study of the conditions and processes that contribute to the flourishing or optimal functioning of people, groups, and institutions" (Gable & Haidt, 2005, p. 104). Hence, the concept of wellbeing, particularly in the psychological sense, is central to its research and applied work.

DOI: 10.4324/9781003415176-2

The Emergence of Positive Psychology

To contextualise the emergence of Positive Psychology, it is essential to delineate its parent discipline, Psychology, and examine the drivers behind its evolution and growth.

Exploring Psychology

Psychology is a scientific discipline defined as the study of behaviour and mental processes (Gleitman et al., 2011). It encompasses a wide range of topics, which can be broadly classified into three aspects of human functioning: cognition – how humans think, emotion – what people feel and behaviours – how individuals and groups act. Psychology scholars explore concepts such as perception, cognition, attention, emotion, motivation, brain functioning, personality, behaviour and interpersonal relationships.

The key branch of psychology is Applied Psychology, a field of practice that uses psychological interventions to treat mental disorders and address common problems of human existence.

Psychology as a scientific discipline encompasses a variety of sub-disciplines, including Personality Psychology, Cognitive Psychology, Social Psychology, Developmental Psychology, Biopsychology, Organisational Psychology, Environmental Psychology, Comparative Psychology and Economic Psychology. Its applied branch includes fields such as Clinical Psychology, Counselling Psychology, Occupational Psychology, Health Psychology, Forensic Psychology, Sports Psychology and Positive Psychology.

The genesis of Positive Psychology as a distinct branch within Psychology largely stemmed as a counteraction to the focus on pathology that dominated Applied Psychology throughout the 20th century. Seligman (1999), the founding leader of Positive Psychology, criticised the field of Applied Psychology for its narrow focus on psychological distress, disorder and dysfunction, and argued that this preoccupation with the negative aspects of human life had led to the narrowing of the field's scope, positioning it primarily as a curative discipline. This limited perspective has left the discipline ill-equipped to harness and leverage the positive aspects of human nature: "Psychology is not just the study of weakness and damage, it is also the study of strengths and virtues. Treatment is not just fixing what is broken, it is nurturing what is best within ourselves" (Seligman, 1999, p. 2). On the back of this critique, Positive Psychology positioned itself as a revolutionary movement that challenged the status quo in Applied Psychology, striving to rebalance the field by attending to positive human attributes in research and practice (Seligman, 2005).

The Mission of Positive Psychology

The objectives of Positive Psychology were ambitiously extensive, aiming "to initiate a shift in psychology's emphasis from solely mending the most detrimental aspects of life to also enhancing positive traits" (Seligman & Csikszentmihalyi, 2000, p. 5). To advance this shift, several pivotal goals were identified (Seligman et al., 2004):

- To place high on the scientific agenda new themes and questions that focus on the healthy aspects of human psychology.
- To devise and empirically test interventions that promote wellbeing.
- To craft a common language that enables communication and understanding of Positive Psychology concepts.
- To combine within therapeutic work positive and negative perspectives and assessments.

Key Topics in Positive Psychology

Rusk and Waters (2013) undertook an extensive mapping of research publications to delineate the range of topics that have been explored within the realm of Positive Psychology in its first 15 years of existence. Their investigation identified 233 concepts, which the authors grouped into 21 broad themes: life satisfaction; happiness; positive emotions; mood; self-efficacy; motivation; self-regulation; creativity; optimism; resilience; hardiness; mental toughness; posttraumatic growth; behavioural change; relationships; altruism; leadership; citizenship behaviour; education; mindfulness and gratitude. The topics that received the most research attention were self-efficacy, happiness, optimism, strengths, engagement and meaning. Among the 233 concepts, 30% are regarded as novel, having emerged after the inception of Positive Psychology. These include constructs such as character strengths, gratitude and psychological capital. In contrast, 70% of the concepts, such as optimism, self-determination and mindfulness, had been studied prior to the establishment of Positive Psychology, therefore prompting questions about ownership. At the outset, the scope of the discipline has been broadly outlined, encompassing these established concepts that are considered allied with Positive Psychology rather than originating from it (Hart, 2020). Furthermore, while many of these topics were examined before Positive Psychology was launched, some had seen limited development over the years. Thus, one of the field's core objectives was to consolidate, acknowledge, prioritise, expand, refine and integrate this body of knowledge (Linley & Joseph, 2004).

Since then, no updated analysis has been conducted. However, a review of recently published textbooks in Positive Psychology (see Boniwell & Tunariu, 2019; Carr, 2022; Compton & Hoffman, 2019; Hart, 2020; Pedrotti et al., 2024; Snyder et al., 2020) indicates that this classification of key themes still holds true.

Interdisciplinary Sub-domains of Positive Psychology

Since its establishment, Positive Psychology has diversified into various directions, some of which have developed into interdisciplinary sub-domains. Each of these sub-disciplines has cultivated its unique theoretical perspectives and applications, while blending with other academic and applied fields. These include two well-established sub-disciplines: Positive Education (Kern & Wehmeyer, 2021) and Positive Work and Organisations (Warren et al., 2017). It also includes a nascent field – Positive Health (Burke et al., 2022) and several emerging domains such as Positive Body (Hefferon, 2013), Positive Ageing (Minichiello & Coulson, 2012), Positive Social Psychology (Roffey, 2011), Positive Neuroscience (Greene & Seligman, 2016), Positive Architecture (Menezes et al., 2021) and Positive Tourism (Filep et al., 2016). It also includes several integrated applied fields: Positive Psychology Coaching (Green & Palmer, 2018), Positive Psychotherapy (Rashid & Seligman, 2018), Positive Cognitive Behavioural Therapy (Bannink & Geschwind, 2021) and Positive Psychiatry (Bannink & Peeters, 2021). One notably absent domain was Positive Economic Psychology, a gap that prompted Hart and Hart (2025) to establish the field.

Limitations and Critique

Positive Psychology has faced substantial criticism, with scholars questioning its philosophical and theoretical foundations, key concepts, research methods and broader implications. A systematic review by van Zyl et al. (2024) identified 117 specific critiques, which the authors categorised into 21 groups under the following overarching themes:

- **Lack of theorisation and conceptual clarity:** Positive Psychology has been criticised for the absence of a unifying meta-theory and distinct philosophical foundations. Further concerns include ambiguous distinctions between "positive" and "negative" experiences, artificial dichotomies and inconsistencies in constructs such as flourishing and wellbeing.
- **Lack of novelty and isolation from mainstream Psychology:** Some scholars argued that Positive Psychology repurposes existing concepts from traditional Psychology without offering substantial innovation. It has also been criticised for isolating itself from the broader discipline and for contributing to the "jingle-jangle fallacy," where different constructs are used synonymously or old ideas are merely relabelled.

- **Methodological issues:** Several methodological critiques have been voiced, including its heavy reliance on self-reports and cross-sectional designs, which limit causal inference and can introduce biases, the focus on individual-level variables, a WEIRD (Western, Educated, Industrialised, Rich and Democratic) (Henrich et al., 2010) population bias, which raises concerns about generalisability, and limited integration of neuroscience and big data approaches. Positive Psychology has also been implicated in Psychology's broader "replicability crisis" (Pashler & Wagenmakers, 2012), with key studies failing to replicate consistently (Brown et al., 2017).
- **Perception as a pseudoscience:** A common critique is that Positive Psychology literature at times lacks sound empirical evidence and relies on unverified claims. Issues such as confirmation bias, tautological reasoning and dependence on "common sense" rather than rigorous scientific methods have been noted.
- **Overcommercialisation:** Positive Psychology has faced criticism for favouring profit-driven interventions over evidence-based practices. Its commercial emphasis on monetising happiness and aligning with consumerist ideologies has raised ethical concerns.
- **Promotion of a neoliberal ideology:** The field has been criticised for prioritising individualism while neglecting systemic and structural factors that shape wellbeing. By conceptualising wellbeing through a neoliberal lens, which emphasises self-reliance and personal responsibility, Positive Psychology overlooks broader societal influences, such as inequality and access to resources.
- **Limited attention to economic and financial aspects:** A particularly pertinent critique for this book is the limited work that pertains to economic and financial aspects of life, beyond the relationship between money and happiness, which has received considerable attention. This critique aligns with the broader disregard of structural and systemic factors that shape wellbeing noted above. Furthermore, key economic indicators – such as income and wealth, consumption, and economic inequality – are largely absent from Positive Psychology research, highlighting a critical area for further exploration.

Hart (2020) noted that while it can be expected that a discipline that challenges the status quo will face fierce critique, some criticisms have been misdirected or exaggerated. Nevertheless, engaging constructively with valid criticisms has encouraged reflection and learning, leading to significant advancements in Positive Psychology's foundational philosophy, theories, methods and interventions.

Lomas et al. (2021) identified three developmental waves within the field: the first wave has taken an oversimplified approach to wellbeing, emphasising the positive side of life; the second attended to the interplay between positive and negative experiences, and the third broadened its scope to incorporate systemic, contextual and interdisciplinary perspectives. Each wave has evolved in response to previous critiques, contributing to the field's growing depth and sophistication.

Conclusion

Positive Psychology has evolved from a corrective movement within Applied Psychology into a substantial and increasingly sophisticated field concerned with the scientific study and practical promotion of wellbeing. Its development has been marked by conceptual expansion, the consolidation of diverse themes and the emergence of interdisciplinary sub-domains that extend its relevance across education, work, health and other areas of life. At the same time, the field's trajectory has been shaped by sustained critique, which has exposed important conceptual, methodological, cultural and ideological limitations. These debates have prompted greater reflexivity and maturation, encouraging scholars to move beyond individualistic and decontextualised accounts of wellbeing towards more nuanced, systemic and interdisciplinary approaches. It is within this more critical and expansive landscape that the present discussion is situated, creating space to consider domains that have remained underdeveloped within Positive Psychology, including its engagement with economic and financial life.

ECONOMIC PSYCHOLOGY

Economic Psychology, a sub-discipline of Applied Psychology and an interdisciplinary field, integrates aspects of Psychology and Economics to examine the impact of psychological factors on economic decisions and behaviours, and vice versa, the influence of economic conditions on individual lives. Ranyard and de Mello Ferreira (2018) defined Economic Psychology as "the science of economic mental life and behaviour" (p. 4). An earlier description by Lea et al. (1987, p. 2) characterised it as "the study of how individuals affect the economy and how the economy affects individuals".

Behavioural Economics

Behavioural Economics emerged as a multidisciplinary field that primarily aimed to develop the field of decision making by incorporating psychological insights into economic models (Ranyard & de Mello Ferreira, 2018). Over time, its focus has expanded beyond decision-making to include financial behaviours, market dynamics and public policy, leading to increased intersection with Economic Psychology. This growing overlap has sparked discussions about the relationship between the two disciplines (Cartwright, 2011). Kirchler and Hoelzl (2018) noted that although Behavioural Economics and Economic Psychology share common intellectual ground and similar objectives, they stem from different traditions: Economic Psychology originated from Psychology, whereas Behavioural Economics is rooted in Economics. Consequently, their distinctions lie in their philosophical foundations, research methodologies and conceptual frameworks.

Despite these foundational differences, the two fields are becoming increasingly intertwined, as Cartwright (2011, p. 11) pointed out: "it seems fair to say that a lot of what has historically been called Behavioural Economics would probably be more appropriately called Economic Psychology". Given this level of convergence, the term Economic Psychology is used in this book as an umbrella term that synthesises elements from both fields.

The Emergence Of Economic Psychology

To understand the unique contribution of Economic Psychology and its emergence, it is important to briefly describe its foundational discipline – Economics.

Exploring Economics

Economics is a scientific discipline that examines the production, distribution and consumption of goods and services (Sloman & Garratt, 2010). It aims to understand the mechanisms of choice-making and the consequences of these choices (whether they are conducted on an individual, household, company, city, state or global level), on the welfare of individuals, companies and societies. Economists study various metrics and indices, such as Gross Domestic Product (GDP), inflation rates, demand and supply, production and consumption, expenditure, economic efficiency, market performance and unemployment, to understand economic performance. They also develop mathematical models to analyse trends and predict future economic activity (Sloman & Garratt, 2010).

The study of economics is divided into two main branches:

- **Microeconomics:** This branch examines the actions of various economic agents, such as individuals, households and companies, and their interactions with different markets. It investigates how these actions and interactions affect the supply and demand for goods and services, influencing prices and market outcomes (Pindyck & Rubinfeld, 2018).
- **Macroeconomics:** This branch examines the economy at an aggregate level, considering the sum total of economic activity and the overarching trends that affect the economy as a whole. It studies phenomena such as inflation, national income, growth and government policies (Blanchard, 2017).

Although theoretically, the concept of financial wellbeing fits under the remit of microeconomics, it has scarcely been explored from a purely economic perspective, and it is commonly investigated from an Economic Psychology perspective (Kaur et al., 2021).

The Goals of Economic Psychology

Economic Psychology originated in the late 19th century, with the influential works of Tarde (1902), who critiqued the lack of psychological insight in Economics. Tarde (1902) posited that economic phenomena cannot be fully analysed, understood or predicted without incorporating a detailed examination of the psychological dimensions of economic behaviour. Therefore, the fundamental aim of Economic Psychology is to apply psychological theories and concepts to investigate and elucidate economic phenomena. It is worth noting that this development occurred soon after Psychology was established as a scientific discipline in 1879, marked by the founding of Wundt's Introspectionist School in Leipzig (Schultz & Schultz, 2011).

A primary goal of Economic Psychology was to examine and challenge the core assumptions underpinning economic theory. Early investigations in the field questioned the concept of "homo economicus", which underlies key economic theories. It suggests that individuals approach economic decisions and actions in a logical and sensible manner, acting on sound information, driven by self-interest and aiming to maximise the utility derived from economic actions (Sloman & Garratt, 2010). The term "utility" is understood as the satisfaction or benefit gained by an individual from their economic decisions or actions (Becker, 1976).

In challenging the concept of homo economicus, Economic Psychology scholars argued that the concept portrays an oversimplified and unrealistic depiction of economic behaviour. To rectify this flaw, they advocated the incorporation of concepts and theories, chiefly from Cognitive Psychology, into the study of economic phenomena. This approach aimed to provide a more realistic representation of economic decisions and behaviours and their causes.

Challenging Homo Economicus: Pioneering Works in Economic Psychology

Below are several examples that illustrate the ways in which scholars in Economic Psychology have contested the underlying assumptions of homo economicus:

- In *The Theory of the Leisure Class*, Veblen (1899) explored the attitudes and lifestyle of US millionaires. His findings on conspicuous consumption revealed how the leisure class indulges in excessive spending to publicly exhibit their economic status, hence indicating a lack of logical judgment in their consumer behaviour. It also underscores the significance of social influences, especially social comparison, in motivating consumption.

- Subsequently, Katona (1951) developed the Index of Consumer Sentiment (ICS), which revealed how people's expectations and attitudes towards the economy affect their decision-making and behaviours, and the irrationality of spending behaviours.
- Around the same time, Simon (1960) observed that business executives often do not seek to maximise profits. Rather, they target specific satisfactory performance levels to ensure their businesses' viability. He coined the term "satisficing" to describe these aspirations, thus shifting the focus away from utility maximisation. His influential work on "bounded rationality" called into question the idea of rationality, which is central to homo economicus (Simon, 1976).
- Tversky and Kahneman's (1974) groundbreaking research on heuristics and biases further challenged the rationality assumption in homo economicus. Their findings showed that individuals frequently use mental shortcuts (heuristics) for economic decision-making, which can result in biases.
- In Prospect Theory, Kahneman and Tversky (1979) argued that people perceive gains and losses differently, often exhibiting risk-averse behaviours. This contradicts the homo economicus assumption of utility maximisation.
- Thaler's (1993) research on economic judgment and decision-making showed that people classify and treat money differently based on its source and purpose, challenging the homo economicus view that decisions are geared to maximise wealth.
- In a subsequent study, Thaler and Shefrin (1981) found that individuals frequently exhibit limited self-discipline, leading to decisions or behaviours that are inconsistent with their long-term interests.
- Lastly, in Nudge Theory, Thaler and Sunstein (2008) proposed that minor alterations in how options are presented to decision-makers can significantly impact their choices and behaviours, which challenges the homo economicus assumption that individuals make choices based purely on rational assessment of existing information.

These examples (and numerous others) illustrate that much of the research in Economic Psychology focused on the ineptitude and ineffectiveness of economic decisions and behaviours, highlighting people's meagre economic literacy, limited capacity for information processing and deficiencies in judgment and decision-making. It also exposed the psychosocial factors that can impede economic thinking and actions, which can lead people to irrational and ineffective economic behaviours. Therefore, a significant critique that could be levelled at this impressive body of work is that, in challenging the key models of Economics, Economic Psychology scholars mainly focused on the negative and deficient aspects of human economic behaviours and experiences, largely overlooking the positive and competent dimensions (Gigerenzer, 2018). A review of recently published textbooks in Economic Psychology (Kirchler

& Hoelzl, 2018; Lewis, 2018; Ranyard, 2018) reveals a persistent focus on maladaptive aspects of economic behaviours, while the adaptive dimensions of human economic behaviour remain under-represented.

Key Topics in Economic Psychology

Economic Psychology covers a wide range of topics, with a stronger emphasis on microeconomics. A review of key themes in papers published in the *Journal of Economic Psychology* between 1981 and 2010 (Kirchler & Hoelzl, 2006, 2018) identified 16 overarching research categories: theory and history; individual decision-making; cooperation and competition; socialisation and lay theories; money, currency and inflation; financial behaviour and investment; consumer attitudes; consumer behaviour; consumer expectations; businesses; marketplace behaviour, marketing and advertising; the labour market; tax behaviours; environmental behaviours; government policy; and other topics. Among these, decision-making and consumer behaviour emerged as the most frequently studied areas.

An analysis of contemporary Economic Psychology textbooks (Ranyard, 2018; Kirchler & Hoelzl, 2018; Lewis, 2018) suggests that these categories continue to represent the core scope of the field. However, it is notable that Kirchler and Hoelzl's (2018) list does not include financial wellbeing, despite the growing academic interest in this area. Similarly, among recently published textbooks, only Ranyard (2018) makes a brief reference to financial wellbeing.

Sub-domains of Economic Psychology

Economic Psychology comprises several sub-disciplines, each dedicated to exploring specific facets of the interaction between psychological processes and economic behaviour. The two principal sub-disciplines of Economic Psychology are Consumer Psychology and Financial Psychology:

- **Consumer Psychology** delves into the psychological underpinnings of consumer behaviour, aiming to comprehend the motivations and consequences of consumption activities conducted by individuals and groups. Research in Consumer Psychology draws on theories and concepts from multiple disciplines, including Psychology, Marketing, Advertising, Sociology and Anthropology, focusing on topics such as motivations, decision-making, perception and attention, information processing, attitudes and the impact of advertising (Jansson-Boyd, 2019).
- **Financial Psychology** applies psychological theories, methods and practices to the areas of personal finance and financial services. Its applied dimension informs the Financial Planning industry, and hence it includes interventions that are designed for client interaction, equipping financial planners with vital skills and tools to help clients attain their financial

objectives (Klontz et al., 2022). It also includes the domain of Behavioural Finance, which applies theories and models from Cognitive Psychology to examine financial behaviours (Klontz et al., 2022). From a research perspective, the field largely relies on surveys, many of which are conducted by the financial industry.

As these descriptions illustrate, there has been scant effort to integrate Positive Psychology with Economic Psychology.

Limitations and Critique

Economic Psychology, like Positive Psychology, has been the subject of considerable debate and controversy. However, discussions within Economic Psychology tend to focus on specific models, empirical findings and methodologies (Cartwright, 2011), rather than broader concerns such as its philosophical foundations, research scope or overall impact.

Key criticisms of Economic Psychology include the following:

- **Lack of overarching theory:** Economic Psychology has been criticised for the absence of a unifying theoretical framework (Fudenberg, 2006). Unlike traditional Economics, which relies on rationality and optimisation as core principles, Economic Psychology focuses on deviations from these norms without an integrated structure to consolidate its findings, hence limiting generalisability and applicability.
- **Lack of novelty:** Some scholars argued that Economic Psychology largely repackages pre-existing concepts from economic literature, such as bounded rationality (Simon, 1960), the costliness of information (Stigler, 1961) and irrational consumer preferences (Galbraith, 1938), offering limited conceptual innovation (McChesney, 2013).
- **Focus on deficits:** Economic Psychology has been criticised for portraying individuals as fundamentally irrational, prone to cognitive biases and easily misled (Gigerenzer, 2015). This perspective suggests that biases are ingrained tendencies, akin to visual illusions, making errors predictable and difficult to correct (Kahneman, 2011).
- **Paternalistic approach:** The field often adopts a libertarian paternalistic stance, using nudges to steer individuals toward "better" decisions, such as saving or healthy eating (Thaler & Sunstein, 2008). Critics have argued that this approach prioritises policymakers' values over individual autonomy and does little to build long-term decision-making skills (Hertwig & Grune-Yanoff, 2021).
- **Methodological issues:** Economic Psychology has been criticised for lacking a distinct methodological identity, and its research methods were described as "eclectic" (Ranyard & de Mello Ferreira, 2018). The extent

of methodological integration between its parent disciplines remains debated, and despite occupying overlapping terrains, key methodological differences between Economic Psychology and Behavioural Economics persist. Although methods from Psychology are subject to similar critiques as those in other psychological sub-disciplines, the heavy reliance on laboratory experiments has been particularly scrutinised over their ecological validity, with concerns that behaviours observed in controlled environments may not generalise to real-world settings (Puce, 2019), and may generate social desirability bias, where participants present themselves favourably in experiments (Zizzo, 2010). The lack of control groups in laboratory studies (Wilkinson & Klaes, 2018) further contributes to methodological criticisms. Additionally, reliance on Western populations and student samples raises concerns about cultural generalisability.

- **Inability to demonstrate causality:** Despite producing abundant documentation of deviations from normative rationality, Behavioural Economics produced little evidence that such deviations lead to economic (or other) losses such as reduced earnings, diminished happiness, poor health or shorter life span (Arkes et al., 2016).
- **Overstated findings:** Critics have argued that the field tends to embrace intuitive results too readily, with selective reporting and publication bias further distorting conclusions (Gigerenzer, 2018).

A particularly relevant critique is the limited exploration of positive and adaptive aspects of economic and financial life. This gap underscores the field's prevailing deficit orientation and highlights an important area for future research.

Conclusion

Economic Psychology has made a vital contribution to understanding economic life by challenging the assumptions of classical economic models and generating rich insights into the psychological processes underpinning economic thinking and behaviour. Yet, despite its interdisciplinary strength and practical relevance, Economic Psychology remains marked by important limitations, including the absence of an overarching theoretical framework, methodological tensions and a persistent emphasis on bias, error and dysfunction. As a result, the field has been far more successful in explaining maladaptive and deficient economic behaviour than in illuminating how individuals and households can think, decide and act effectively in economic life. This imbalance points to a significant conceptual and empirical gap and suggests the need for a more integrative perspective that brings the study of competent and wellbeing-enhancing economic functioning into clearer focus.

POSITIVE ECONOMIC PSYCHOLOGY

Positive Economic Psychology is an interdisciplinary scientific discipline that integrates Positive Psychology and Economic Psychology. It is primarily concerned with researching and promoting financial and economic wellbeing, focusing on the conditions and processes that can foster economic prosperity and optimal economic functioning in individuals, groups and institutions. Thus, the concept of financial and economic wellbeing is fundamental to its research and applications (Hart & Hart, 2025).

In this context, financial wellbeing is defined as a construct applicable at the individual and household level, whereas economic wellbeing pertains to broader entities such as organisations, communities and nations.

The Emergence of Positive Economic Psychology

The establishment of Positive Economic Psychology as a distinct field arose in response to Economic Psychology's historical focus on economic challenges and deficits. A review of the pioneering books that have shaped the field's development, such as *Heuristics and Biases* (Gilovich et al., 2002), *Predictably Irrational* (Ariely, 2008), *Misbehaving* (Thaler, 2015), *Noise* (Kahneman et al., 2021), *Why Smart People Make Big Money Mistakes and How to Correct Them* (Belsky & Gilovich, 2010) and *Nudge* (Thaler & Sunstein, 2008), exposes an entrenched perception among scholars that people are ill-equipped for sound financial decision-making and prudent financial behaviours, as Klontz et al. (2022, p. 16) noted: "we are not wired to make good decisions with money". This perspective suggests that the flaws in economic judgment and decisions, and the deficiencies and errors in economic behaviours, are largely innate, stemming from cognitive and psychosocial limitations.

Reflecting the development of Positive Psychology (Seligman, 1999), Positive Economic Psychology aims to broaden the scope of Economic Psychology beyond its preoccupation with financial and economic inadequacies and dysfunctions. Hart and Hart (2025) argued that the excessive concentration on the adverse aspects of economic thinking and behaviour has resulted in a significant scholarly gap: there is scarce academic research on prudent and productive economic behaviours, evidence-based strategies for wealth building or ways to overcome the cognitive and psychosocial shortcomings identified by Economic Psychology scholars. This gap has been largely filled by the self-help industry, which often lacks empirical evidence to back its recommendations and interventions.

This critique, therefore, positions the creation of Positive Economic Psychology as a corrective movement within Economic Psychology. It aims to offer a more holistic and balanced perspective on economic thought and behaviour by integrating both the positive and negative aspects. Its goal is to recalibrate the field, placing emphasis on research and applied practices that not only tackle economic and deficiencies, but also actively pursue evidence-based approaches to enhance economic wellbeing and prosperity.

The Mission of Positive Economic Psychology

The mission of Positive Economic Psychology is ambitiously wide-ranging: to initiate a shift in Economic Psychology from its current focus on the negative and dysfunctional aspects of economic life, to investigate and promote positive economic functioning and abundance. To facilitate this transformation, several key aims were proposed (Hart & Hart, 2025):

- To introduce new themes and questions into the scientific agenda, focusing on the positive and proficient facets of economic behaviour and decision-making.
- To create and empirically test micro-level strategies and interventions that foster financial wellbeing.
- To develop and implement meso and macro-level policies that encourage effective and prudent economic behaviours and promote financial and economic wellbeing in individuals, households and organisations.
- To examine, address and reduce economic hardship and disparities in economic opportunities and outcomes across diverse groups.
- To formulate a common language that can aid the communication and understanding of concepts within Positive Economic Psychology.
- To incorporate both positive and negative perspectives and evaluations in the context of economic counselling and financial planning.

The Principles of Positive Economic Psychology

Hart and Hart (2025) outlined several principles that establish the scope, philosophical stance, objectives and primary focus areas of Positive Economic Psychology.

- **Positive assumptions about human nature in economic contexts:** Research and applied work in social sciences often build upon underlying assumptions about human nature, entailing implicit value judgements. Traditional and Neoclassical Economics have been influenced by the concept of homo economicus, which depicts people as rational economic agents, primarily driven by self-interest and the maximisation of personal gain. While Economic Psychology initially aimed to contest these assumptions by uncovering the complexity of human economic behaviour (Kahneman, 2011), an analysis of its agenda indicates a subtle yet pervasive negative view of human nature, which focuses on people's inherent economic shortcomings, ignorance and incompetence, leading to economic dysfunction and poor outcomes.

In contrast to both fields and similar to Positive Psychology (Seligman, 2005), Positive Economic Psychology draws from Aristotelian and Humanistic traditions. It therefore perceives individuals as driven by a natural propensity for economic growth and prosperity, and capable of sensible, ethical and effective economic decisions and behaviours. This view also holds that with deliberate awareness and effort, individuals can surmount the innate cognitive and psychosocial economic limitations identified by Economic Psychology scholars.

- **Positive aim:** The primary objective of Positive Economic Psychology, in alignment with Positive Psychology (Pawelski, 2016), is to examine and unpack the components and drivers of positive, adaptive, efficient and satisfying economic behaviours and decision-making processes.
- **Positive agenda:** Following the principles of Positive Psychology (Pawelski, 2016), this point highlights the key themes or subjects that are fundamental to the field, such as financial wellbeing, abundance, economic resilience, happiness, optimism, grit, self-regulation, economic intelligence and financial wisdom.
- **Positive processes:** This point relates to the mechanisms or strategies that Positive Economic Psychology seeks to implement, often as part of its interventions. Similar to Positive Psychology (Sin & Lyubomirsky, 2009), these processes aim to develop or utilise skills that enable individuals and groups to achieve their economic objectives and experience economic growth and prosperity. Examples include attaining economic knowledge, experience or literacy, exercising self-discipline, self-awareness or mindfulness and contesting money beliefs and biases.
- **Focus on applications:** The goal of Positive Economic Psychology is to create interventions that foster beneficial economic outcomes such as financial wellbeing, prosperity and economic resilience. Therefore, in alignment with Positive Psychology (Parks & Biswas-Diener, 2013), it applies a research-driven approach to nurture a life of abundance.
- **Non-clinical target population:** This facet defines the primary target population that Positive Economic Psychology aims to serve, which predominantly focuses on individuals who are categorised as non-clinical. This target demographic is analogous to that of Positive Psychology (Pawelski, 2016).
- **Constructive lexicon:** In line with its assumptions about human nature, the terminology of Economic Psychology often includes terms that imply economic ineptness or impediments, such as biases, ignorance, limitations, denial, dependence, distortions, noise, conflict, crisis, irrationality, incongruence, laziness, loss, error, fraud, abuse and financial disorders (see for example Kahneman, 2011; Thaler, 2015; Klontz et al., 2022). In alignment with Positive Psychology (Maddux, 2005), Positive Economic Psychology aims to cultivate a more balanced discourse through its

vocabulary. Its goal is to enable the expression, exploration and discussion of the positive facets of human economic psychology. Within this framework, cognitive limitations and ineffective economic behavioural patterns are construed as common life challenges that can be addressed and surmounted, rather than undefeatable obstacles destined to result in economic mistakes or failures.

- **Non-directive value position:** As an applied psychological discipline, Positive Economic Psychology adopts a non-directive and non-paternalistic approach, avoiding prescriptive advice. Aligned with Positive Psychology's humanistic roots, it emphasises a self-determined approach designed to empower individuals to exercise their agency, and offers resources and strategies to help people achieve their personal economic goals (Linley et al., 2006). This stands in contrast to the approach taken particularly in Behavioural Economics, which adopts a libertarian paternalistic perspective (Thaler & Sunstein, 2008), designed to gently "nudge" individuals towards more beneficial decisions and actions, hence applying a directive approach.

As we shall see in the forthcoming chapters, these principles feature strongly in the contemporary work on financial wellbeing.

Current Developments

Several research domains which blend elements from Economic Psychology and Positive Psychology align with the scope of Positive Economic Psychology. Prominent examples include the domain known as Happiness Economics (Easterlin, 2004; Agrawal et al., 2023), which has produced a large volume of work on the association between money and happiness. In many of the recent publications, "happiness" is defined and measured in accordance with Positive Psychology conventions as "subjective wellbeing", and recent research in this domain has incorporated significant insights drawn from the research in Positive Psychology (Tay et al., 2018).

Another significant research theme is optimism, especially in business settings. While early work in Economic Psychology viewed optimism as a cognitive bias (Kahneman & Tversky, 1996), in a later review of the topic, Kahneman (2011) drew on an extensive body of research conducted by Positive Psychology scholars on the benefits of optimism (Carver & Scheier, 2001; Seligman, 2006) and argued that "when action is needed, optimism, even if the mildly delusional variety, may be a good thing" (Kahneman, 2011, p. 256).

Another approach that is consistent with the Humanistic viewpoint of Positive Psychology is "boosting strategies" proposed by Hertwig and Grune-Yanoff (2017, 2021). This approach seeks to strengthen individuals' abilities to make autonomous decisions and choices. In contrast to nudging strategies, which subtly steer choices by altering the decision environment (Thaler &

Sunstein, 2008), boosting strategies concentrate on empowering individuals to utilise their own agency. These strategies include educational and psychoeducational interventions, as well as various forms of guidance and consultancy, providing tools and techniques to enhance individual competence and self-sufficiency in economic settings.

An additional example is financial wellbeing. Inspired by the distinctions made in Positive Psychology between hedonic and eudaimonic aspects of psychological wellbeing (Hart, 2020), Salignac et al. (2020) contended that financial wellbeing incorporates both dimensions and defined financial wellbeing as "how happy people are with their current financial situation, and their ability to function economically" (Salignac et al., 2020, p. 1583).

Lastly, Klontz et al. (2022) encouraged the use of several Positive Psychology interventions (such as optimism and gratitude) in the context of financial planning.

These examples (and several others) indicate that the amalgamation of concepts from Positive Psychology and Economic Psychology is already underway. The emerging discipline seeks to recognise these areas and offer them a conceptual home.

Future Possibilities and Challenges

We are currently in an era where interdisciplinarity is shaping the research landscape. Scholars frequently explore opportunities at the intersection of multiple disciplines and funding bodies increasingly recognise that addressing complex societal challenges requires research that transcends traditional disciplinary boundaries (Lyall et al., 2011). However, interdisciplinary research involves more than simply merging different fields into a single project. It requires considerable effort to foster synergy and cultivate a community of experts who can integrate specialised knowledge across disciplines.

Common challenges in interdisciplinary research include navigating distinct philosophical, linguistic and methodological traditions that shape how knowledge is constructed and communicated. Overcoming these differences requires fostering mutual understanding among scholars from diverse fields, yet this process is often hindered by entrenched biases, disciplinary silos and resistance to change. Additionally, critiques from established disciplines, scepticism regarding the legitimacy of a new field and concerns about its positive orientation and efforts to rebalance traditional perspectives may further complicate progress.

Despite the growing emphasis on interdisciplinarity, there remains limited research on effective strategies for facilitating collaboration and knowledge integration across disciplines. Consequently, a key challenge in establishing a new interdisciplinary field – particularly one that synthesises insights from multiple domains, such as Economics, Psychology, Economic Psychology and Positive Psychology – is the necessity of stepping beyond well-established disciplinary conventions and navigating uncharted intellectual territory.

By building on the strengths and addressing the limitations of its parent disciplines, Positive Economic Psychology is well-positioned to integrate and enhance its contributions across three key domains:

- **A balanced view of human capabilities:** Economic Psychology has traditionally focused on deficits, such as irrational decision-making, financial mismanagement and the negative consequences of economic behaviours. This has led to a predominantly pessimistic view of human capabilities. In contrast, Positive Psychology emphasises strengths, potential and growth, though it has been criticised for being overly idealistic. Positive Economic Psychology aims to synthesise these perspectives, acknowledging the cognitive biases and systemic barriers identified in Economic Psychology while also recognising the capacity of individuals, organisations and communities to develop adaptive and effective financial behaviours.
- **A broadened scope:** Positive Psychology has been critiqued for its focus on intra-individual factors, such as personal strengths, optimism and resilience, while paying less attention to structural and systemic influences, such as economic inequality and access to resources. Conversely, Economic Psychology adopts a multi-level approach, addressing influences at the micro, meso and macro levels. It also incorporates significant research on external factors that shape financial and economic outcomes, including market dynamics, policy frameworks and socioeconomic conditions. Positive Economic Psychology seeks to integrate these approaches, offering a holistic perspective that balances personal agency with structural realities across multiple levels of analysis.
- **Novel interventions:** Positive Economic Psychology aims to bridge the applied focus of Positive Psychology with the behavioural insights of Economic Psychology to develop innovative strategies for enhancing financial and economic wellbeing. While Positive Psychology has created numerous interventions to promote wellbeing, resilience and other positive outcomes, Economic Psychology has largely focused on understanding financial behaviours rather than developing practical tools to influence them. The financial planning industry has stepped into this void with the creation of financial interventions. By integrating these approaches, Positive Economic Psychology aspires to design interventions that not only foster adaptive financial behaviours but also address maladaptive patterns. These interventions extend beyond individuals to empower communities and systems, promoting ethical financial practices and equitable access to resources.

While the challenges of integrating diverse disciplinary perspectives and establishing a new academic field are significant, they present opportunities for innovation and intellectual growth. By fostering collaboration across disciplines and embracing both the strengths and limitations of its parent fields,

Positive Economic Psychology has the potential to offer a more holistic and balanced framework for addressing real-world economic challenges.

Conclusion

This chapter examined the emerging field of Positive Economic Psychology, situated at the intersection of Positive Psychology and Economic Psychology. Its distinctive contribution lies in its focused commitment to enhancing financial and economic wellbeing through interdisciplinary research and practical application. Positive Economic Psychology aims to address key gaps in both parent disciplines by advancing underexplored concepts, introducing novel psychological constructs and developing innovative interventions supported by rigorous measurement tools.

What sets Positive Economic Psychology apart is its foundational assumption about human nature – viewing individuals as inherently capable of making sound, ethical economic decisions and driven by intrinsic motivations for growth, prosperity and prosocial contributions. Unlike the deficit-oriented perspectives and libertarian paternalistic approach often found in Economic Psychology, Positive Economic Psychology employs constructive terminology, reframing financial challenges as manageable and highlighting human strengths and potential. It also adopts a non-directive stance, avoiding prescriptive approaches to how individuals should manage their economic lives. Its positive agenda promotes adaptive financial behaviours, responsible organisational practices and policies that empower both individuals and communities. By fostering a strengths-based approach to economic life, Positive Economic Psychology offers a transformative pathway toward financial prosperity and broader human flourishing.

Looking ahead, Positive Economic Psychology is set to experience significant growth and influence. Nonetheless, it confronts several challenges, such as ensuring methodological precision in integrating varied approaches, fostering interdisciplinary cooperation and remaining relevant to real-world economic issues.

Positive Economic Psychology represents a bold and innovative approach to understanding the intersection of human wellbeing and economic behaviour. While its future trajectory appears promising, it requires careful steering to develop into a robust, impactful and truly transdisciplinary field.

3 Money Matters

The multifaceted concept of money has long intrigued scholars across various disciplines, serving as both a pivotal component of economic systems and a fundamental element of individual and societal wellbeing. Money encompasses a wide array of financial instruments and assets, each playing a unique role within the broader economic landscape. Understanding these forms and their respective functions is crucial for grasping the complexities of financial interactions and transactions that underpin economic stability and growth.

This chapter seeks to establish a foundation for examining financial wellbeing by delving into the complex nature of money. It begins with a definition of money and an exploration of its history. Subsequently, the chapter investigates the various financial concepts discussed in the literature on financial wellbeing, such as income, wealth, consumption, socioeconomic status, poverty and inequality, and introduces the common methodologies used for measuring these factors.

MONEY: A HISTORICAL PERSPECTIVE

In today's world, people have grown accustomed to the presence of money, making it difficult for most of us to imagine a society without cash, credit cards or digital transactions. Historically, money was introduced about 3,000 years ago to replace the barter trading system in which goods or services were exchanged for other goods or services (Martin, 2014). While the creation of money addressed many of the drawbacks and limitations associated with barter, it also introduced a critical psychological change. In the barter system, both parties were required to agree on what is fair and determine the value and quantity of one product against another. It also required individuals to understand and accommodate each other's needs and desires, and therefore necessitated consideration, responsiveness, interpersonal negotiation skills and cordiality (Morgan, 1969). The barter system, therefore, fostered social connection and interdependence (Ostroy & Starr, 1990). However, the necessity of understanding and satisfying each other's needs, referred to as the "double coincidence of wants", was both time-consuming and often frustrating (Ostroy & Starr, 1990).

DOI: 10.4324/9781003415176-3

The introduction of money allowed individuals to acquire the goods and services they needed without the requirement for close social interactions, thereby making trade more efficient and flexible. But at the same time, the use of money introduced a new social dynamic, whereby people could concentrate on their own desires, needs and goals, without having to consider what others need or might find useful. Hence, it fundamentally transformed commercial relations from an other-oriented to a self-oriented transaction, fostering a sense of independence and disconnection from others, which had significant social and psychological implications. Morally, the move towards a self-oriented system can lead to prioritising personal gains over collective needs, raising ethical concerns about the impact of economic transactions on social cohesion and social support (Weatherford, 1998). The psychological shifts brought about by the introduction of money, along with its influence on our perspectives and relationships, continue to echo to this day (see section on money priming below).

Conceptualising Money

Historically, money was created to facilitate commercial transactions by serving as a standardised medium of exchange. However, to fully comprehend its role, researchers have explored several critical questions: What exactly is money? What are its key functions within economic systems and in people's lives? What role does the state play in the management of monetary systems?

Money Frameworks

Two influential economic theories illuminate the nature and function of money. Each offers a distinct conceptualisation of money, but holds different assumptions about money's origin, purpose and value, thereby providing essential foundations for understanding both its economic and sociopolitical functions.

The Commodity Theory of Money

The earliest conceptualisation of money is attributed to Aristotle (1255/1984), who defined money as a commodity that facilitates economic exchange. Drawing on Aristotle's ideas, Smith (1776) and Ricardo (1817) developed the Commodity Theory of Money, which maintains that money is an economic instrument that fulfils four key functions:

- **Medium of exchange:** Money acts as an intermediary instrument used to facilitate the sale, purchase or trade of goods between parties (Mankiw, 2021).

- **Unit of account:** Money provides a common measure of value, which simplifies the comparison and valuation of diverse goods and services. This function aids in standardising economic transactions and in accounting practices (Mishkin, 2016).

- **Store of value:** Money allows individuals and businesses to preserve wealth over time. It therefore must hold its value (at least in the short term), enabling deferred consumption and investment (Samuelson & Nordhaus, 2010).

- **Standard of deferred payment:** Money is accepted as a means to settle debts that are payable in the future, thus facilitating credit transactions and financial planning (Krugman & Wells, 2018).

Despite continued critique, the Commodity Theory of Money definition can be found in numerous contemporary economics textbooks (Mankiw, 2021; Parkin, 2011). An obvious flaw of this theory is that it has difficulties in explaining inflation and the decreasing value of money over time (Keynes, 1936). An additional critique of this model is that it conceptualises money as an instrument, and hence, from an economic point of view, money cannot become an end in itself. However, this raises the question of whether this perspective adequately captures the role that money plays in people's lives (Marx, 1887).

The State Theory of Money

An alternative definition, based on the State Theory of Money (also known as Chartalist or the State Theory of Money), views money as a tool created by the state to facilitate commercial transactions (Innes, 1914). It represents a promise from one party to deliver a product or service to the money holder (Ingham, 2004).

For this function to be effective, two essential features are required:

- The promise must be credible, indicating that the money issuer is creditworthy.
- The credit should be transferable, indicating that all parties will accept it as a means of payment.

In this theory, the state plays a central role in legally defining what is accepted as money, and this endorsement gives money its value. The theory emphasises the role of government policies and social agreements in shaping the monetary system, and argues that money cannot be fully understood without considering the social, political and legal contexts in which it operates.

Money Priming

Money Priming is an intriguing example of the ways in which money can impact people's cognitions, emotions and subsequent actions. Money Priming Theory posits that exposure to money-related stimuli (such as images of cash, words related to money or physical handling of money) influences individuals, often in subconscious ways, and can activate a wide range of cognitive and emotional responses that affect how people act (see reviews by Vohs, 2015; Stajkovic et al., 2022). Examples of these effects include the following:

- **Enhanced performance:** Money priming can make people more motivated, self-regulated and focused, work harder and be more persistent.
- **Increased agency and focus on the self:** Research has shown that when people are primed with money, they tend to feel a heightened sense of agency, independence, autonomy and self-efficacy, and become more self-sufficient. However, they also become more self-centred and more focused on their personal goals and aspirations.

Figure 3.1 Images of cash

- **Materialistic attitudes:** Money priming can reinforce materialistic attitudes and values, making individuals more likely to prioritise wealth and possessions over other aspects of life, such as relationships and personal growth.
- **Changes in decision-making:** Exposure to money can alter decision-making processes, making individuals more likely to engage in unethical activities, risk-taking behaviours and make decisions that favour short-term gains over long-term benefits.
- **Increased social distance:** Money priming can increase psychological and physical distance from others. People reminded of money tend to show a reduced inclination to engage in community activities and a greater desire for personal space. They also tend to be more distant and indifferent in their social interactions, feel less interdependent and display lower empathy and compassion towards others.
- **Reduced prosocial behaviours:** Money priming often leads to a decrease in prosocial behaviours, such as helping others, volunteering and donating to charity. Studies have found that individuals exposed to money-related cues are less likely to engage in acts of kindness and more likely to prioritise their own interests over those of others.

Money priming is a powerful psychological phenomenon that influences a wide range of attitudes and behaviours, often in subtle ways. The effects of money priming have significant implications for various fields, including marketing, organisational behaviours and public policy.

Conclusion

The evolution of money has not only transformed economic systems but also reshaped social relations and psychological orientations. From barter to digital assets, money has increased economic efficiency and autonomy, while also fostering individualism and altering social values. Theoretical frameworks like the Commodity and State Theories of Money illuminate its structural roles, yet a psychological lens is essential for understanding its broader impact. Research on topics such as money priming demonstrates how even subtle cues can influence cognition, behaviour and relationships. Far from being a neutral tool, money is a powerful symbol with material and psychological consequences that merit deeper interdisciplinary attention.

INDIVIDUAL FINANCIAL RESOURCES

Research on financial wellbeing explores diverse micro-level financial resources that individuals and households hold, including income, wealth, assets, debts, investments and consumption. Together, these concepts provide a comprehensive picture of the financial state of a person or a household, capturing present ability to satisfy needs, future planning capacity and the prospect of stability and growth. Understanding these elements is essential for unpacking and researching financial wellbeing, and for developing effective policies or interventions aimed at improving prosperity and reducing economic disparities.

Income

Income is a fundamental concept in Economics since it affects consumer behaviour, savings, investment and economic stability. It also plays a crucial role in research in determining poverty levels, standard of living, economic inequality and social mobility. Policymakers use income data to design tax policies, social welfare programmes and other economic strategies to promote growth and reduce hardship (Mankiw, 2021).

Income refers to the monetary compensation received by an individual or a household, typically derived from various sources such as wages from employment or self-employment, business profits, investments and other financial gains.

Income can be categorised into the following types:

- **Earned income:** Salaries and private pensions.
- **Investment income:** Dividends and interest.
- **Passive income:** Rental income and royalties.
- **State support:** State pension, child benefit and other types of state support.
- **Other sources:** Family support, grants, alimony and other sources.

Measures of Income

Income data is typically collected on gross annual income, either at the individual or at the household level (Shrider & Creamer, 2023). To calculate gross annual income, all types of income are aggregated into one sum, which includes earnings from employment, state support, interest from savings or investments, dividends, rental income, royalties, grants, alimony and other sources. In some studies, however, income is calculated as net income (post-tax income).

Regardless of whether gross or net income data is collected, questionnaires commonly present income brackets and require participants to select the bracket that applies to them. Subsequently, researchers often use the midpoint of the selected bracket to estimate individuals' income.

When household income data is collected, researchers calculate the income of each adult in the household, using various methods that differ across studies.

Some studies examine changes in income over time, which require following up households for several years, measuring yearly incomes and then calculating changes that occurred during this period (Frijters et al., 2020)

Although income is frequently seen as the most straightforward measure of an individual's financial resources, accurately collecting income data is a complex task. It necessitates careful consideration of the wording of questionnaire items, assessment of the quality of data provided by participants, meticulous data computation and analysis and prudent interpretation of the findings.

Wealth

Wealth encompasses the total value of an individual's or a household's financial and non-financial assets, excluding any liabilities. It includes physical assets (such as property, vehicles and household goods), financial assets (such as savings, investments, insurances and pensions), as well as intangible assets (such as intellectual property). It also takes into account all liabilities (mortgages and other debts).

The comprehensive nature of wealth makes it a crucial indicator of an individual's economic stability and capacity to endure periods of financial volatility, thus playing a vital role in the assessment of financial wellbeing. Beyond personal financial stability, wealth is also a critical factor in economic mobility, social inequality and economic stability on a national level, highlighting its broader societal implications (Hansen, 2014).

Although seen as distinct, income and wealth are interconnected in several ways, which make the attempt to assess them independently challenging.

Income can contribute to wealth accumulation through savings, pension schemes and investments. Equally, wealth can generate income via returns on savings and investments, supplementing or replacing earned income from employment (Davies, 2011). Income and wealth are also linked in their contribution to sustaining a household's lifestyle over time. Income determines a household's consumption capacity, while wealth provides stability during periods of low income, ensuring that living standards can be maintained despite income fluctuations (D'Ambrosio et al., 2020). Wealth also allows for investment in education, training and health, thereby enhancing an individual's earning potential and future income (Becker, 1964). An important point to highlight is that throughout a person's life stages, the balance between income and wealth shifts: younger individuals may rely more on income, while older individuals may draw more on their accumulated wealth (Cagetti, 2003).

Measures of Wealth

Wealth is calculated by summing the market value of all physical and intangible assets of a household and subtracting from this sum the value of liabilities to derive a total net wealth figure. Assets include property, contents, vehicles, private pension, investments and savings. Liabilities include mortgages, loans and credit card debt (ONS, 2018, 2022).

Due to the complexity involved in collecting the detailed data required for calculating wealth, studies tend to gather data on one or a few of the components of wealth (for example: assets, investments, pensions, savings or debt), which are then used as proxies for an individual or a household's wealth. These can be assessed through eliciting the monetary value of these assets, or through self-report questionnaires that invite respondents to evaluate the state of their debt, investments, savings and insurances.

Few studies examined changes in net wealth over time, looking at overall gains and losses either in assets, liabilities or both (Uppal & LaRochelle-Cote, 2015).

In some studies, subjective measures of wealth were applied. For example, Gasiorowska (2014) asked participants to assess their financial situation. Another item asked about participants" ability to make ends meet. Both were assessed on a 1–5 scale. It is worth noting, however, that these items do not directly assess wealth.

As can be seen, collecting accurate wealth data can be challenging, which might explain the use of proxies and subjective measures.

Consumption

Consumption is defined as the process through which individuals, households and organisations choose, acquire, use and dispose of goods and services to satisfy their needs and desires (Solomon, 2020).

Consumption is a crucial economic activity, essential for the functioning and growth of an economy. It also constitutes a fundamental aspect of individuals' lives, influencing the satisfaction of basic needs. However, most people do not consume solely for practical purposes. Research indicates that consumption and possessions have evolved into a means of self-expression – an extension of the self, through which people construct and display their identities, values, aspirations, social affiliations and status (Belk, 2018). In this context, material goods play a pivotal role in shaping individuals' psychological and social experiences. A robust body of evidence suggests that consumption has become a key pathway through which individuals pursue wellbeing and happiness (Ahuvia, 2018; Dhiman & Kumar, 2023).

Measures of Consumption

Most surveys on consumption use self-report questionnaires that require participants to report on their households' spending during a defined period on particular categories of goods and services (such as food and beverages, clothing, housing, utilities, equipment, health, transportation, communication, recreation, education and financial services). Then, drawing on this data, the percentage of spending on each category is calculated. An example of a questionnaire that is commonly used to elicit this type of data is the Personal Consumption Expenditure questionnaire (BEA, 2023), which can be adjusted for different locations and currencies.

Similar ways to collect data were employed in studies that differentiated between utilitarian and hedonic purchases (Babin et al., 1994), and those that assessed relational consumption (Tsurumi et al., 2021) and lifestyle consumption (Farrag et al., 2010). In these studies, participants are either asked to assess how much they spend on average in a month on these consumption categories or to report what percentage of their monthly consumption budget is spent on particular types of goods or services.

Researchers also developed particular questionnaires to assess other consumption categories, such as buying material possessions or experiences (Howell et al., 2012), whether money is spent on oneself or on others (Aknin et al., 2012), consumption that is geared towards saving time (Whillans et al., 2016), conspicuous consumption (Roy-Chaudhuri et al., 2011), compensatory shopping (Sidra, 2025), impulse buying (Verplanken & Herabadi, 2001), loyal shopping (Kursunluoglu, 2014), environmentally friendly consumption (Quoquab et al., 2019), consumption within the sharing economy (Warwas et al., 2022), online and instore shopping (Cao et al., 2012), ethical consumption (Delistavrou & Tilikidou, 2012) and customer involvement (Laurent & Kapferer, 1985).

Data on consumption patterns are necessary for understanding how consumption is associated with different aspects of individuals' wellbeing and are also essential for companies. Kotler and Keller (2016) highlighted the importance of understanding consumers' choices, decision-making processes and buying behaviours. Marketers routinely collect data on consumption behaviours and can use these insights to gain a competitive advantage over their rivals (Smith, 2019). However, as seen in the description of consumption measures, gathering accurate data on consumption is an intricate task, riddled with challenges. Although the integration of big data into consumption research holds promise for enhancing data quality, its application remains limited at present.

Conclusion

Absolute individual financial resources – income, wealth and consumption – contribute uniquely to the understanding of financial wellbeing. Income supports daily living expenses and savings, while wealth reflects the total assets individuals can rely on for long-term security and resilience against financial shocks. Consumption patterns, in turn, reveal how resources are allocated and the lifestyle standards achieved. Together, these elements provide a comprehensive view of a person or a household's financial health, offering insights into their ability to manage present financial needs and future stability.

Despite their importance, accurately measuring income, wealth and consumption remains challenging (see critique below). While these financial concepts offer valuable insights, it is important to approach their interpretation with an awareness of their limitations, striving towards more nuanced approaches to understanding financial resources.

RELATIVE CONCEPTS

Relative concepts like poverty, socio-economic status (SES) and relative income or wealth offer comparative perspectives on a person's or a household's financial state and wellbeing. While absolute measures such as income and consumption provide straightforward but limited data, relative concepts consider an individual's financial situation within its broader societal context, hence accounting for disparities and social stratification. Focusing on relative measures helps researchers understand socioeconomic dynamics and inequality, offering a more contextualised view of financial resources.

Poverty

Poverty is defined as a multifaceted socio-economic condition marked by a significant dearth of financial resources and material assets, which hinders individuals or groups from achieving a basic standard of living. Its key indicator is the insufficient financial means to satisfy essential needs such as food, shelter, clothing and healthcare (World Bank, 2022).

Poverty has garnered increased research interest across multiple disciplines, including Psychology. Recent data indicate that approximately 700 million people worldwide live in extreme poverty, accounting for about 9.2% of the global population (World Bank, 2022). In the EU, around 21% of people live in poverty (Kalinowski & Rosa, 2021), while in the US, the poverty rate is approximately 11% (Creamer et al., 2022). Alarmingly, recent reports suggest that poverty is on the rise (World Bank, 2022).

Psychological research has demonstrated that deprivation affects individuals' physical and mental health (Marbin et al., 2022).

Research into the causes and consequences of poverty, as well as into strategies for alleviation, necessitates the use of diverse research methods and interdisciplinary collaborations, with psychological perspectives playing a pivotal role (Bullock, 2019).

Measures of Poverty

Poverty can be assessed through objective or subjective measures:

- **Objective measures** require the collection of data on income, wealth or expenditure (as detailed earlier) and comparing these to a national poverty threshold. Poverty is determined when a household's income, assets or expenditure falls below the threshold (DHH, 2024). Another approach to measuring poverty is by gathering data on the receipt of state support (Adelman et al., 2000).
- **Subjective poverty measures** elicit individuals' perceptions of their economic situation and their sense of material deprivation. The UK Income Evaluation Question, for example (Flik & Van Praag, 1991), presents the following items: "How many pounds a week, after tax, do you think

are necessary to keep a household such as the one you live in, out of poverty"? This is followed by: "How far above or below that level would you say your household is"? (with answers ranging between 1 – a lot below that level of income, to 5 – a lot above that level of income).

Measuring poverty is crucial for several reasons. Accurate poverty measurement is essential for understanding its scope, addressing its causes and improving the quality of life for those affected by it. It enables governments and organisations to design and implement policies and social welfare programmes (World Bank, 2022). Understanding the extent and nature of poverty helps allocate resources where they are most needed and craft targeted interventions. Measuring poverty also allows for the assessment of progress over time, providing benchmarks against which the effectiveness of policies and programmes can be evaluated, ensuring accountability and guiding future actions. Standardised poverty measurements also facilitate international comparisons, helping to identify global trends, share best practices and coordinate efforts to combat poverty on a larger scale. Importantly, identifying and measuring poverty allows societies to acknowledge the presence of inequality and recognise our moral obligation for social justice, thereby raising awareness and motivating collective efforts to reduce poverty and improve living standards. Lastly, measuring poverty can empower marginalised communities by giving them visibility and a voice, highlighting their struggles and mobilising support for their rights and needs (Jolliffe & Prydz, 2021).

Socio-economic Status

Socio-economic status (SES) is a relative concept that reflects an individual's or group's social and economic standing within society. It is utilised across numerous disciplines and encompasses several key dimensions: income, education and occupation, which collectively influence access to resources and opportunities. It is therefore not considered an economic concept solely.

Socio-economic status is defined as the social standing or class of an individual or group along a social stratification system. As a scientific concept, it assesses a person's capacity to access essential resources such as education, work, healthcare, housing, nutrition, leisure, information, technology, social networks and political systems (Saunders, 2006).

Socio-economic status measures are used for various purposes across different fields due to their impact on many aspects of life. For example, in the realm of medical research, SES is used for understanding health disparities in access to healthcare and health outcomes, helping to identify areas necessitating intervention (Adler et al., 1993). In Education, SES addresses educational inequalities and informs the development of policies and programmes that aim to provide equal opportunities for students from diverse backgrounds (Sirin, 2005). Economists utilise SES to study economic behaviours, market trends and the distribution of wealth. It aids in understanding consumer behaviour, labour market dynamics and the effects of economic policies (Piketty, 2014). In Psychology, SES is used to explore its effects on mental health, cognitive development and behaviour, providing a deeper understanding of how socio-economic factors contribute to stress, self-esteem, wellbeing and happiness (Yu & Williams, 1999).

Policymakers also rely on SES data to design and implement social policies aimed at reducing poverty, improving economic opportunities and promoting social welfare. It guides decisions on taxation and welfare programmes, making it a foundational element in policymaking (Duncan & Magnuson, 2012). Similarly, SES is vital for examining social mobility, shedding light on the opportunities available for individuals to improve their socio-economic standing and the barriers that hinder upward mobility (Wilkinson & Pickett, 2010).

Measures of Socio-economic Status

SES can be evaluated using objective or subjective measures:

- **Objective measures of SES:** Objectively, SES is commonly measured using education, income and occupation data, reflecting its multidimensional nature. These components can be evaluated separately or combined into a composite index. However, many studies gather only data on one of these indicators, which is then used as a proxy for SES (Saunders, 2006).
- **Subjective measures of SES:** Subjective SES is mainly assessed using scales that allow individuals to rank their own socio-economic position relative to others (Kraus et al., 2012). The MacArthur Scale of Subjective Social Status (Adler et al., 2000) is a widely used measure for this purpose. The scale uses a pictorial format with a 10-rung social ladder, and respondents are asked to indicate their socio-economic standing compared to others in society, based on income, education level and occupation.

SES is an indispensable tool for gaining insights into the socio-economic dimensions of human life, with a particular focus on context, relative standing and social disparities. It guides research, informs policy and addresses inequalities, making it a cornerstone in efforts to understand and improve various aspects of society.

Relative Income and Wealth

Relative income refers to an individual's or household's income compared to the income of their reference group, which could be others in the same social group, a geographic community or a nation (Boyce et al., 2010).

Similarly, **relative wealth** refers to the comparison of an individual's or household's accumulated assets, liabilities and net worth, to that of their reference group (Pfeffer & Schoeni, 2016).

The concepts of relative income and wealth highlight the comparative nature of financial resources, focusing on how the financial state of an individual or a household measures up against others, rather than their absolute income or net worth. These concepts are rooted in the theory of social comparison (Festinger, 1954), which posits that individuals assess their social and personal worth by comparing themselves to others, thereby evaluating their abilities, achievements and status in relation to their peers. Further research also found that engaging with social comparison, particularly around financial resources, impinges on people's wellbeing (Boyce et al., 2010).

Measures of Relative Income and Wealth

Relative income and wealth can be assessed through objective or subjective measures:

- **Objective evaluation:** Following the collection of data on income or wealth (as described above), researchers can assess relative income or wealth in two ways: comparing an individual's income or wealth to their reference group through calculating percentile ranking, or through ratio comparisons (Ball & Chernova, 2008).
- **Subjective evaluation:** Another way to assess relative income or wealth is to elicit individuals' self-evaluation of their position compared to others through subjective ranking questionnaires. For example, Layard et al. (2010) asked participants to compare their income with that of their reference group, rating the differences on a 1–5 point scale (lower/higher than average). Another commonly used scale uses a 10-rung ladder ranging from the poorest households to the richest in one's community and requires participants to locate the rung that best describes their state (see, for example, Caso et al., 2025).

Similar to the constructs of poverty and SES, measuring relative income and wealth provides vital insights into social disparities and, more importantly, how the perceptions of disparities affect individuals' economic experiences and wellbeing.

Conclusion

Relative concepts such as poverty, relative income, wealth and socio-economic status (SES) offer a critical lens on financial wellbeing by situating individuals within a broader societal context. Unlike absolute measures, they highlight disparities and social stratification, revealing how differences in financial resources shape wellbeing and access to opportunities. These insights are key to developing policies that promote equity and inclusion.

However, relative measures face challenges: their meaning can shift across time and place, and subjective assessments may be shaped by personal and cultural perceptions, complicating comparisons (see critique below). Despite this, they remain essential for understanding the links between financial resources, inequality and wellbeing.

MACRO LEVEL CONCEPTS

Understanding state and global level economic concepts is crucial for analysing the economic health and development of nations, as well as for assessing how the national or global economic contexts affect the financial state and wellbeing of individuals, communities and organisations.

Gross Domestic Product (GDP) serves as a fundamental indicator of a country's economic performance, while the Human Development Index (HDI) adds depth by including health, education and income to assess the overall quality of life of a population. Measures of economic inequality further reveal disparities in wealth and income distribution. Together, these indicators provide a comprehensive view of a country's economic status and development.

Gross Domestic Product

> **Gross Domestic Product** (GDP) is a vital economic indicator that measures the total monetary value of all goods and services produced in a country over a specific time period (Mankiw, 2021). As a country-level concept, it serves as a broad measure of a nation's overall economic activity and strength.

Policymakers, economists and analysts rely on GDP data to assess economic growth and guide fiscal and other policy decisions (Krugman & Wells, 2018). An increase in GDP over time indicates a healthy economy with increasing production and consumption, while a decline in GDP can signal economic difficulties. By evaluating GDP, decision-makers can determine if an economy is expanding or contracting, which helps in planning and implementing strategies to foster economic stability and growth. Comparing GDP across countries can offer insights into the relative economic strengths and weaknesses of a country, which has repercussions for international trade, investments, aid allocation and influence on global affairs.

In the context of research on financial wellbeing, the use of GDP enables researchers to compare countries and evaluate how different economic environments affect individuals' financial outcomes and wellbeing.

Measuring GDP

There are three primary approaches to measuring GDP (Landefeld et al., 2008):

- **The production (output) approach** calculates GDP by summing up the value of output produced by each sector (such as agriculture, manufacturing and services), after subtracting the cost of goods and services used in production.
- **The income approach** measures GDP by summing all gross profits of companies, wages paid to employees and taxes, minus subsidies on products.
- **The expenditure approach** calculates GDP by adding up all expenditures in the economy, including household consumption, business investments, government spending and net exports, minus imports.

From these national measures of GDP, per capita GDP can be calculated by dividing the overall GDP for the country, by the number of citizens.

Human Development Index

The Human Development Index (HDI) is a composite statistic used to rank countries based on human development levels, integrating three key dimensions: health, education and standard of living (Baumann, 2021).

The HDI was developed by the UN Development Programme to provide a broader measure of development than GDP, which captures economic output but not overall wellbeing and quality of life (UNDP, 2024). By incorporating health, education and living standards, the HDI shifts attention from economic growth to whether people have opportunities to live healthy, educated and prosperous lives. It also enables cross-country comparisons, helps to identify best practices, highlights areas of weakness and supports more effective policy and resource allocation. In addition, the HDI serves as an advocacy tool by underscoring the importance of integrating human wellbeing into development strategies.

HDI Measures

The Human Development Index (HDI) is calculated by integrating three essential dimensions of human development (Baumann, 2021):

- **Health:** Measured by life expectancy at birth, this dimension reflects the ability to live a long and healthy life.
- **Education:** Assessed through two indicators – mean years of schooling for adults aged 25 years or more, and expected years of schooling for children entering school, this dimension gauges access to knowledge and education.
- **Standard of living:** This aspect requires calculating the average gross income per capita for the country. This figure is then adjusted for Purchasing Power Parity (ensuring that income assessment is comparable across different countries by accounting for variations in cost of living and inflation rates). This dimension reflects the ability to maintain a decent standard of living.

A country's HDI score is calculated as the mean of the three components, which is then normalised to yield a value between 0 and 1, with higher values indicating higher levels of human development (Baumann, 2021).

The HDI provides an indicator of development at a country level, prompting researchers to assess the relationship between HDI and various aspects of wellbeing, including happiness, a topic that has gained considerable interest in recent decades (Roka, 2020).

Economic Inequality

Economic inequality refers to the unequal distribution of financial resources between individuals or groups within a society. The literature refers to two primary types of economic inequality: income inequality (Piketty, 2014) and wealth inequality (Saez & Zucman, 2016).

Economic inequality has become a prominent issue in recent decades, marked by a significant rise in disparities in income, wealth and access to opportunities across the globe (Milanovic, 2016). This growing gap has been attributed to factors such as globalisation, technological advancements and the erosion of social and welfare policies (Piketty, 2014).

Measuring Inequality

Inequality can be measured through objective or subjective measures. Most measures of economic inequality are macro-level measures that aim to offer a comparison between countries.

- **Objective measures** include the Gini index (and similar measures), which assess income or wealth inequality within a country. It is often used to compare the level of inequality across countries. It ranges between 0 and 1, with lower scores indicating greater equality and higher scores indicating increased inequality (Cowell, 2011).
- **Subjective measures** of economic inequality capture individuals' perceptions of the income or wealth distribution within their society or within their close social circle:
    - **The Subjective Inequality Scale** (Schmalor & Heine, 2022) is an example of a subjective measure. It includes eight items that capture how equitable individuals believe the economic system in their country is, and how justly they think income and wealth are distributed. Answers are ranked on a 1–7 Likert agreement scale, and a total score is calculated by aggregating all items.
    - **The Perceived Economic Inequality in Everyday Life** (Garcia-Castro et al., 2019) includes 12 items that elicit people's views on how they compare to their social group. Example items include: "Among the people I surround myself with, some people can afford to buy a lot more and better things than others". Items are marked on a 1–7 Likert agreement scale and then summed up to derive a total score.

Psychological research into economic inequality has demonstrated its effects on psychological wellbeing, consumption patterns, social cohesion, sense of injustice, social unrest, trust, corruption and numerous other aspects (Wilkinson & Pickett, 2010; Easterbrook, 2021; Wei et al., 2023; Velandia-Morales et al., 2022).

Conclusion

Macro-level economic concepts like GDP, HDI and economic inequality offer crucial frameworks for assessing the economic health and development of nations. GDP reflects economic activity, while HDI adds health and education to offer a broader view of human development. Measures like the Gini index expose income and wealth disparities, highlighting social imbalances within and between nations. Together, these concepts allow for a richer understanding of how national and global economic environments shape the financial wellbeing of individuals and communities.

Despite their utility, these macro-level measures face significant critiques (see details below). Nonetheless, they remain vital tools for understanding economic contexts, guiding policymakers and researchers in their efforts to promote equitable and sustainable development.

Limitations and Critique

Income, wealth, consumption, poverty, SES, relative income and wealth and broader economic indicators, including GDP, HDI and economic inequality, contribute to our understanding of the interplay between financial resources, whether individual or societal, and financial wellbeing, offering various lenses through which this dynamic can be explored and understood. However, significant critique has been levelled at these economic concepts and measures, highlighting limitations that can undermine their reliability.

- **Data inaccuracy:** Both micro and macro data, whether absolute or relative, can be prone to inaccuracies. For instance, data on income, wealth and consumption often depend on individuals' ability to accurately recall or assess their income from various sources, the market value of their assets and their typical and atypical expenditures. Likewise, poverty, relative income and wealth data may be unreliable due to difficulties in comparing one's assets to their reference group. This challenge is exacerbated by factors such as individual mobility, multiple residences, citizenships and varying reference groups. Measures of economic inequality, like the Gini coefficient, also heavily depend on accurate and comprehensive income data. However, in many countries, data on income and wealth distribution are incomplete or unreliable. Moreover, inequality metrics tend to focus on income rather than wealth, even though wealth inequality is more pronounced and provides a longitudinal perspective on economic disparity. Additionally, economic inequality measures frequently overlook non-economic dimensions of inequality, such as access to healthcare, education and social capital, which are critical to overall wellbeing and social mobility.
- **Limited meso-level constructs and measures:** The financial wellbeing literature rarely engages with meso-level financial concepts (such as

organisational or community-level financial indicators), which explains their absence from the preceding sections. This points to a notable gap in the field regarding how such meso-level factors may influence the financial wellbeing of individuals and households, and conversely, how individual and household financial wellbeing may affect the financial capacities of organisations and communities.

- **Underreporting and misreporting:** Absolute and relative individual data often suffer from underreporting or misreporting, particularly among high-income and high-wealth participants who may have incentives to hide information to avoid taxes (Piketty, 2014).
- **Use of proxies:** While the most effective way to assess a person's financial resources is by considering income, wealth and consumption together, this comprehensive approach is rarely used. Many studies primarily collect income data, using it as a proxy for overall financial resources. Additionally, due to the complexity of gathering wealth data, researchers often resort to collecting information on debt or savings as a stand-in for wealth. Similarly, when assessing socio-economic status, proxies are commonly employed, with researchers frequently relying on just one component (income, education or occupation). This can result in an incomplete representation and potentially misleading conclusions.
- **Obstacles in comparing data across studies:** Due to the varied methods used to collect data on income, wealth, consumption, SES, relative income and wealth and poverty, making comparisons across studies is fraught with challenges and inaccuracies, which necessitates careful attention as to what was measured and compared.
- **Subjective measures:** Subjective assessments of wealth, SES, relative income or wealth, poverty or inequality are influenced by the very context they aim to capture. These can introduce biases in participants' responses that researchers are unable to fully account for, making it challenging to establish consistent benchmarks.

Absolute Concepts and Measures

- **Exclusion of informal economy:** Consumption, income and wealth measures often exclude transactions that occur in the informal economy, which can be substantial, especially in developing countries, leading to an incomplete picture.
- **Exclusion of non-monetary assets:** Income and wealth measures typically exclude non-monetary income, such as in-kind benefits (e.g., health insurance, food assistance), which can be significant for low-income households.

Relative Concepts

- **Lack of concepts that describe sufficiency or affluence:** While considerable effort has been dedicated to developing measures of poverty, there are no universally accepted benchmarks for assessing financial sufficiency or affluence (Castro & Bleys, 2023).
- **Context dependency:** Relative measures of income and wealth depend on the specific population and time period that one is being compared to, which can lead to different interpretations of discrepancies and may not capture long-term trends effectively.

Macro Level Concepts

- **Limited scope:** GDP is often critiqued for its inadequacy in measuring overall welfare and quality of life. While it quantifies economic activity, it does not account for the distribution of income among residents of a country, nor does it consider non-market transactions, environmental degradation or social factors that contribute to wellbeing (Stiglitz et al., 2009). GDP also includes activities that may have negative impacts, such as deforestation or pollution, without deducting the costs associated with these activities. This can lead to a misleadingly positive picture of the economic health of a country.
- **Masking disparities:** The HDI measure is based on three dimensions: life expectancy, education and per capita income. Critics argue that the index is too narrow and does not capture other important aspects of human development, such as inequality, poverty and security (Klugman et al., 2011). The HDI also aggregates data into a single composite index, which can mask disparities within countries. For instance, two countries with the same HDI score might have vastly different distributions of health, education and income within their populations (Anand & Sen, 1994).

These limitations show that economic concepts and indicators provide valuable but partial representations of the financial conditions that shape financial wellbeing. Although measures such as income, wealth, consumption, poverty, socio-economic status, relative financial position, GDP, HDI and inequality each illuminate important aspects of material life, they are constrained by data inaccuracy, underreporting, proxy use, context dependency and limited comparability across studies. At both the micro and macro levels, many of these measures simplify complex realities, overlook informal and non-monetary resources, mask internal disparities and fail to capture broader social, relational and contextual factors that influence how financial resources are experienced. The neglect of meso-level constructs further suggests that the field has not yet adequately addressed the ways in which financial wellbeing is embedded within organisations and communities. Advancing scholarship in this area requires greater methodological precision, clearer distinctions between related constructs, more comprehensive and context-sensitive assessment strategies and stronger integration across levels of analysis in order to develop a fuller understanding of the relationship between economic conditions and financial wellbeing.

Conclusion

This chapter set out to establish a foundation for understanding financial wellbeing by examining the diverse dimensions of financial resources. It began with a definition of money and moved on to explore a range of financial constructs. At the micro level, it considered income, wealth, consumption, relative income and wealth, poverty and socioeconomic status; at the macro level, it examined broader indicators such as GDP, HDI and economic inequality. Each of these contributes valuable insights into economic behaviour and societal development, revealing the connections between individual resources, their wider economic context and their financial wellbeing.

Yet, the limitations and biases embedded in these measures are significant. Critiques of these indicators highlight the need for a more nuanced approach to assessing financial resources, one that recognises and seeks to address their shortcomings. By understanding both the strengths and the constraints of existing frameworks, we can gain a more comprehensive view of the complex factors that shape financial wellbeing.

4 Wellbeing and Happiness

Wellbeing is an inherent human objective, reflecting the desire to satisfy our needs, achieve our life goals and lead a balanced, harmonious and fulfilling life. Positive Psychology epitomises the concept of wellbeing through the experience of "life well lived", which encompasses two key components: feeling good and functioning well (Hart, 2020). But what does the term "good life" mean? This question has sparked lively debates for decades, and scholars still disagree on what is the optimal combination of factors that encapsulate wellbeing (Lomas et al., 2024).

On the back of this age-old debate, this chapter lays the foundation for exploring financial wellbeing by exploring its parent concept – overall wellbeing and its vital component – happiness. The chapter begins by defining wellbeing. It then unpacks the principal components of wellbeing: hedonic and eudaimonic wellbeing. The following section delves into the concept of overall wellbeing, reviewing key models and measures. The chapter then examines happiness by conducting a parallel analysis.

CONCEPTUALISING WELLBEING

Wellbeing is a dynamic and multifaceted concept explored by numerous disciplines, each contributing unique insights. While it is deeply rooted in Psychology, particularly in Positive Psychology, the past two decades have seen a surge of interest across various fields, including Sociology, Social Work, Economics, Public Health, Medicine, Business, Education, Environmental Studies, Anthropology and Political Science. This multidisciplinary interest has given rise to numerous constructs, synonymous terms and diverse interpretations of wellbeing, its dimensions and components, reflecting the richness of the field. However, it also highlights the lack of consensus around crucial points, which generates misunderstandings and attracts repeated critique (see the limitations section below).

DOI: 10.4324/9781003415176-4

The concept of **wellbeing** conveys the idea of a "life well lived" (Hart, 2020, p. 47) and is viewed as a central human aspiration, involving the fulfilment of needs, the pursuit of personally valued goals and the experience of a balanced, meaningful and satisfying life. Lomas et al. (2024, p. 8) defined overall human wellbeing as a continuum reflecting "the relative attainment of a personal subjective state of quality". This suggests that wellbeing can be seen as an individual's subjective assessment of the extent to which they have achieved an optimal quality of life and level of functioning. The term "quality" denotes a level of goodness.

The concept of "flourishing" represents the attainment of a high level of wellbeing.

The Components of Wellbeing

Positive Psychology scholars often describe wellbeing as comprising two core elements: **feeling good** and **functioning well** (Deci & Ryan, 2008). These dimensions are grounded in two longstanding philosophical traditions (Huta & Waterman, 2014):

- **Hedonia** (or hedonic wellbeing) refers to the experience of pleasure, satisfaction and gratification. It is generally understood as the experiential facet of wellbeing, and, in current research, is often seen as synonymous with happiness.
- **Eudaimonia** (or eudaimonic wellbeing) refers to the behavioural aspect of wellbeing, encompassing effective functioning across varied life domains, the enactment of virtues, engagement in worthy pursuits and the realisation of one's potential.

The distinction between hedonia and eudaimonia is often traced to Aristotle, who used the term *eudaimonia* to describe a life worth living: a way of life through which a heightened state of quality and value can be attained (Huta, 2016). For Aristotle, eudaimonic wellbeing was central to the good life and was explicitly distinguished from hedonia (Henderson & Knight, 2012). At the same time, hedonic experience was recognised as a state that arises from eudaimonic living and functioning (Huta, 2016). This interpretation gave rise to a major divide in the wellbeing literature, with hedonia and eudaimonia treated as distinct concepts, a division that has remained especially influential in Psychology.

With the emergence of Positive Psychology, empirical research on both constructs expanded substantially. This work has consistently pointed to a strong association between hedonia and eudaimonia (Goodman et al., 2017). Their relationship has also been characterised as bidirectional: the extent to which people function well shapes how happy they feel, while happiness can in turn support more effective functioning (Pavot & Diener, 2004). This body of evidence has contributed to an emerging view that overall wellbeing encompasses both hedonic and eudaimonic elements, each of which is essential to a fulfilling life (Lomas et al., 2024).

Following years of debate, the hedonia–eudaimonia distinction has become firmly established in the wellbeing literature and has spread across disciplines. It is now widely regarded as a leading meta-theoretical perspective that offers a valuable lens for understanding the components of wellbeing. Even so, models that break these broad dimensions down into more specific elements differ in the extent to which they incorporate and integrate both elements.

OVERALL WELLBEING

Overall wellbeing is an umbrella construct that captures how well a person is faring as a whole, integrating multiple life domains. It can be defined as "the quality of one's personal subjective state across the physical, mental, social, and spiritual dimensions of existence" (Lomas et al., 2024, p. 11).

A person's general wellbeing is typically assessed subjectively by integrating several life domains into a single overall indicator. Within this perspective, domains such as physical, psychological, social, occupational and financial wellbeing reflect key areas of functioning, experience and subjective evaluation. Each domain represents a distinct sphere of life in which resources, demands, opportunities and constraints influence how well a person is faring.

At the same time, substantial variation exists in how scholars and practitioners define and organise these domains. There is no clear consensus on what should be included, which domains should be considered core, or how many are needed to adequately capture overall wellbeing (see critique section below).

Models of Overall Wellbeing

Models of overall wellbeing break the construct down into a set of constituent domains (e.g., psychological, social, physical and occupational), each capturing a distinct aspect of living well. These models are often accompanied by measures that assess hedonic dimensions (such as positive affect or life satisfaction) and eudaimonic dimensions (related to functioning within each domain), and then combine domain-level scores into an overall index. Although such approaches differ in their theoretical assumptions and in the number and the scope of the domains they include, they share a common purpose: to offer a coherent framework for understanding overall wellbeing and a practical basis for its measurement and comparison. The following section presents two illustrative examples drawn from models currently in use.

The Gallup Wellbeing Model

The Gallup Wellbeing Model is among the most widely used frameworks in large-scale survey research. Gallup's long-running programmes, including the World Poll, which was launched in 2005 and has been administered in more than 140 countries, have made it possible to examine patterns of wellbeing both across countries and over time.

The model identifies five domains of wellbeing that may be examined individually or combined into an overall composite score. These domains are assessed through individuals' subjective evaluations of their wellbeing in each area, capturing both eudaimonic and hedonic aspects of wellbeing (Rath & Harter, 2010):

- **Career wellbeing:** This domain relates to everyday activities, especially work and other productive pursuits, and to the fulfilment and sense of purpose derived from engaging in them.
- **Physical wellbeing:** This component concerns the maintenance of health and vitality, which underpin effective daily functioning and the capacity to accomplish tasks.
- **Social wellbeing:** Reflecting the importance of relationships for wellbeing, this domain concerns the presence of supportive and meaningful connections, as well as experiences of love and belonging.
- **Community wellbeing:** This aspect refers to a person's interest in, participation in and engagement with community life and civic affairs at local and/or national levels.
- **Financial wellbeing:** This domain focuses on managing one's finances in ways that minimise hardship and financial stress while promoting feelings of stability and security.

The Gallup Wellbeing Scale

To summarise overall wellbeing, Gallup developed a set of benchmarks designed to help individuals evaluate their current levels of functioning and contentment, identify less developed areas and reflect on possible routes for improvement (Rath & Harter, 2010). The approach generates a score from 0 to 100 for each of the five domains and applies predefined thresholds to differentiate more optimal from less optimal levels of wellbeing. On the basis of these scores, Gallup groups overall wellbeing into three categories:

- **Thriving:** Individuals in this category report strong functioning across domains and are more likely to experience positive day-to-day states, such as feeling well-rested, enjoying their daily activities and experiencing comfort. Thriving is defined by scores of 70 or above.
- **Struggling:** This category indicates moderate functioning in one or more domains, alongside more frequent experiences of stress and everyday challenges. Struggling corresponds to scores between 40 and 69.
- **Suffering:** Individuals in this category report low levels of functioning and poor daily experiences across most or all domains, with scores below 40. Gallup's findings link this profile to difficulty meeting basic needs, poorer physical health and greater psychological distress.

Overall Wellbeing: Global Evaluation

The Gallup State of Global Wellbeing report (2014) presented a sobering picture: across each facet of wellbeing, only one in four people were classified as thriving, most were struggling and a significant minority fell into the suffering category. More recent evidence from the Gallup Global Life Evaluation Index (2024) indicated that global wellbeing has shifted only marginally over the past two decades. On average, 28% of people were classified as thriving, 60% were categorised as struggling and 12% were marked as suffering, suggesting a pattern that has remained broadly stable worldwide.

These global averages, however, conceal considerable regional and national variation. Western countries tend to report higher levels of thriving and lower levels of suffering across wellbeing domains, likely reflecting differences in economic security, healthcare systems and institutional support. Nevertheless, despite increasing public awareness of wellbeing and the introduction of wellbeing-focused policy interventions, the relative stability of the global distribution of wellbeing implies that existing approaches have not produced substantial improvements in wellbeing.

It is important to note that the survey format and item content have been revised periodically for methodological reasons, and this should be taken into account when interpreting trends across waves. The index nonetheless provides a pragmatic and policy-relevant approach to conceptualising overall wellbeing as a multidimensional and subjective construct that integrates both hedonic and eudaimonic elements.

The OECD How's Life Wellbeing Framework

The OECD's (2017) How's Life? framework conceptualises overall wellbeing by distinguishing between people's experienced wellbeing and the broader macro-level conditions needed to sustain wellbeing over time. Within this framework, wellbeing is organised into 11 dimensions:

Material living conditions:

- **Income and wealth:** The financial resources available to households, including both income and accumulated wealth, which can help smooth consumption over time.
- **Housing:** Access to adequate shelter, safety, privacy and personal space, together with the wider residential environment that shapes access to services and opportunities.
- **Work and job quality:** Participation in employment and the quality of working conditions, encompassing both material features (such as pay, job availability and security) and non-material features (such as the work environment).

Quality of life:

- **Health:** Being physically fit and feeling well, including living a long life free from physical or mental illness and being able to engage in valued activities.
- **Knowledge and skills:** What people know and are able to do, reflecting capabilities developed through education and life experience.
- **Environmental quality:** The condition of the natural environment, which affects health through factors such as air, water and soil quality, and is also valued intrinsically through access to nature.
- **Work–life balance:** The extent to which people are able to combine work, family responsibilities and leisure, including both how time is allocated and how it is experienced.
- **Social connections:** The quantity and quality of social relationships and interactions, including time with family and friends, access to and availability of support and satisfaction with one's relationships.
- **Civic engagement and governance:** The degree to which people participate in civic life and are able to influence decisions affecting their society.
- **Safety:** Freedom from harm, including risks associated with crime, violence, conflict, terrorism, oppression, accidents and natural disasters.
- **Subjective wellbeing:** Overall life satisfaction and the balance of positive and negative affect.

In addition, the framework considers a set of macro-level conditions as the foundations of sustainability, which determine whether a country can maintain or improve wellbeing over time:

- **Economic capital:** The stock of produced assets (including infrastructure, buildings, machinery and intellectual property) together with financial assets and liabilities that support economic activity and material living standards.

- **Human capital:** People's skills and capabilities (including education and tacit knowledge), alongside health (encompassing physical and mental wellbeing). These are valued both in their own right and for their contribution to other wellbeing outcomes.
- **Natural capital:** A country's natural resources and ecosystems, ranging from minerals and timber to oceans and the atmosphere, as well as the services they provide. These are tracked through indicators of their current state, changes over time and associated risks and resilience factors.
- **Social capital:** The norms, shared values and institutional arrangements that facilitate cooperation and collective action, often reflected in indicators such as interpersonal trust and the quality of governance.

Because national averages can obscure substantial disparities, the framework also considers inequality in three ways:

- **Horizontal inequalities:** Differences between population groups.
- **Vertical inequalities:** Gaps between those at the top and bottom of the distribution within each dimension.
- **Deprivations:** The proportion of the population falling below minimum thresholds of achievement.

The OECD How's Life Measure

The OECD (2017) How's Life questionnaire contains 24 items and captures both objective and subjective indicators, as well as hedonic and eudaimonic aspects, across the various dimensions of wellbeing. The results may be examined for each domain or aggregated into an overall wellbeing score. Example items include "How is your health in general?" (rated on a 1–4 scale from poor to very good) and "If you were in trouble, do you have relatives or friends you can count on to help you whenever you need them?" (with yes/no response options). Responses are summed and recoded to produce an index score ranging from 1 to 100.

The OECD How's Life framework is among the few comprehensive models of wellbeing that combine a multidimensional perspective on people's current quality of life with a forward-looking focus on the national capital stocks that support the sustainability of wellbeing over time. In addition to identifying core wellbeing domains, the framework incorporates extensive financial data, draws on both objective and subjective indicators and encompasses both hedonic and eudaimonic dimensions of wellbeing.

How's Life in OECD Countries

The recent OECD (2024) report evaluated post-pandemic recovery, concluding that although policy responses helped buffer many of the pandemic's economic effects, recovery remains incomplete, particularly in non-material and sustainability aspects of wellbeing.

Material conditions improved across OECD countries, with disposable household incomes protected and employment recovering. However, the recovery has been uneven, with weak real wage growth and widespread perceptions of financial strain. Housing affordability and financial insecurity were identified as major vulnerabilities, intensified by inflation and rising living costs. Since 2019, the proportion of low-income households has risen in around one-third of OECD countries, with nearly one in five lower-income households spending more than 40% of their income on housing. Energy poverty also increased, with around 1 in 11 people reporting that they are unable to keep their homes adequately warm.

Recovery in non-material wellbeing and resilience has been weaker, and in some cases, negative. Subjective and social outcomes deteriorated, with nearly 30% of people reporting frequent experiences of physical pain, worry and sadness. Trends in life satisfaction were mixed, while loneliness ranged from 4% to 14% across countries.

Looking ahead, the report points to growing risks to natural and social capital, including slower progress on recycling and protected areas, worsening biodiversity, greater exposure to extreme heat and declining institutional trust.

Overall, OECD countries appear to have recovered economically, but this has not been matched by comparable progress across other dimensions of wellbeing.

Several shared commitments are evident across these models. Both models conceptualise wellbeing as multidimensional, breaking it down into distinct domains such as work, health, relationships and finances, and thereby allowing both domain-specific assessment and overall scoring. They also combine, in different ways, hedonic components with eudaimonic components, reflecting the now widely accepted view that wellbeing cannot be reduced to happiness alone. At the same time, they differ in emphasis. Gallup presents a more streamlined model centred on five domains and a strong reliance on self-reported evaluative measures, whereas the OECD framework is broader in scope, linking individual-level outcomes with macro-level conditions for long-term sustainability.

Conclusion

Wellbeing is best understood as a dynamic, multidimensional state that reflects how individuals evaluate and experience the quality of their lives across key domains, such as health, relationships, work and finances. It is a rich and evolving construct that bridges philosophical traditions, disciplinary perspectives and methodological approaches. The long-standing distinction between hedonia (feeling good) and eudaimonia (functioning well) continues to shape theoretical and empirical work, yet recent research increasingly supports an integrative view in which both dimensions are essential for a fulfilling life.

Building on this foundation, contemporary models of overall wellbeing attempt to capture its multidimensional nature through a variety of models and measures. While challenges remain in achieving definitional and measurement consensus, the diversity of tools and frameworks underscores the importance of context-sensitive, holistic approaches to wellbeing assessment. These insights provide a crucial backdrop for the subsequent exploration of financial wellbeing, which is best understood as a component within the broader structure of overall wellbeing.

HAPPINESS

The pursuit of happiness has been a driving force in our collective psyche, shaping our desires, our actions and even our societies. In the US, the Declaration of Independence (1776) established specific constitutional rights for citizens that governments are obliged to protect. Chief among these rights are "life, liberty, and the pursuit of happiness." Since then, surveys conducted across various cultures and generations have found that people consistently rate happiness as a highly desirable goal, viewing it as both attainable and sustainable (Diener et al., 1999). However, some scholars argued that the emphasis on happiness in the political and public discourse represents a modern obsession (Burnett, 2011).

But what is happiness? Is it a fleeting moment of joy, a cognitive evaluation, a sustained sense of contentment or a personality trait? Scholars from various fields have grappled with these questions, each offering unique insights. Measuring happiness presents its own set of challenges. How do we quantify something so deeply personal and subjective? Over the years, researchers have crafted numerous tools to capture the essence of happiness.

Conceptualising Happiness

In academic texts, happiness is often referred to as *hedonic* or *subjective wellbeing* (SWB) (Diener, 2000), which comprises two main components:

- **Cognitive component:** This aspect involves evaluating one's life satisfaction overall or within particular life domains.
- **Emotional component:** This facet captures the frequency of experiencing positive emotions and negative emotions during a specified period.

Subjective wellbeing is frequently represented by the following formula:

SWB = Satisfaction with life + Positive affect − Negative affect

By definition, individuals with high levels of subjective wellbeing are likely to be satisfied with their lives, experience positive emotions frequently and experience negative emotions infrequently (Diener, 2000). The experience of positive emotions, therefore, lies at the core of happiness, which is why it is frequently regarded as synonymous with hedonia (Huta, 2016).

Capturing these facets of happiness, Hart and Hart (2026) defined happiness as a continuum that involves an individual's global appraisal of life alongside a person's emotional experiences.

Happiness and Wellbeing

Within contemporary wellbeing science, happiness is conceptualised as the hedonic dimension of wellbeing, concerned with how positively life is experienced and evaluated, thereby complementing eudaimonic wellbeing, which emphasises the quality of a person's functioning within and across life domains.

Happiness Overall and within Life Domains: Bottom-Up, Top-Down and Bi-directional Theory

Happiness can refer to how satisfied a person feels with specific areas of life, such as work, health or relationships, or to their overall sense of life satisfaction. Early research treated global life satisfaction as a sum of satisfaction across key life domains, a view known as the **bottom-up theory** (Headey, 2024). This perspective suggests that external life circumstances, such as financial stability and a satisfying relationship, build up to form overall happiness. It has underpinned much of the policy and economic interest in promoting wellbeing by improving living conditions. However, research findings challenged this view, as they demonstrated that factors such as income or marital status explain only a small proportion of the variance in happiness, and many major life events were found to have limited long-term effects on happiness (Lyubomirsky et al., 2005).

These limitations led to the emergence of **the top-down theory**, which holds that people's overall life satisfaction influences how they perceive specific life domains. In this view, those who are happier tend to see their lives through a positive lens (Nakazato et al., 2011). This approach is supported by perspectives which propose that happiness levels are partly heritable and, hence, to some degree stable (Lyubomirsky et al., 2005).

Together, these perspectives offer two ways of thinking about how to promote happiness: by changing external circumstances (bottom-up) or by changing internal dispositions and perceptions (top-down). In practice, both matter. A growing body of research supports a **bidirectional model**, in which life satisfaction and domain satisfaction influence each other, with changes in one feeding into and shaping the other (Malvaso & Kang, 2022).

The Measures of Happiness

- **Subjective wellbeing measures**

  Research into happiness often employs self-report questionnaires to measure the two components of subjective wellbeing: satisfaction with life and individuals' emotional experiences:

  - **Life satisfaction measures:** Two questionnaires are often used to assess life satisfaction:
    - **The Cantril Self-anchoring Scale:** Commonly presented as a ladder, this measure (Cantril, 1965) features one item: "Overall, how satisfied are you with your life nowadays"? Answers are scored on a 0–10 evaluation scale.
    - **The Satisfaction with Life Scale (SWLS):** This scale (Diener et al., 1985) includes five items, scored on a 1–7 agreement Likert scale. Example items include: "The conditions of my life are excellent. These are summed up to derive an overall score."

  - **Emotions measures:** To evaluate participants' emotional experiences, researchers often utilise one of the following questionnaires:
    - **The Positive and Negative Affect Schedule (PANAS):** This inventory invites participants to rate the extent to which they experienced 20 emotions (ten positive emotions, such as interested and excited, and ten negative emotions like distressed and upset) within a specific time period (Watson et al., 1988).
    - **The Scale of Positive and Negative Experience (SPANE):** This measure includes 12 broad positive and negative emotional categories (such as positive/negative, happy/sad) (Diener et al., 2010).

In both scales, answers are recorded on a 1–5 frequency scale. Scores are then summed up separately for positive and negative emotions. Affect balance can be calculated by subtracting the negative emotions score from the positive emotions score.

One of the key challenges in subjective wellbeing measures is that life satisfaction and emotion measures cannot be combined into a composite score and are therefore analysed and presented separately. Consequently, researchers often use one of the components of subjective wellbeing as a proxy for happiness, a practice that has attracted significant critique (see below). This challenge has prompted the development of additional scales designed to produce a unified score for happiness.

- **Unified happiness measures:**
  - **The UK Census:** This commonly used measure includes a single question: "Overall how happy did you feel yesterday"? Responses are scored on a 0–10 scale (ONS, 2023).
  - **The Subjective Happiness Questionnaire:** This measure (Lyubomirsky & Lepper, 1999) includes four items beginning with the prompt: "In general, I consider myself." Participants rate their state on a 1–7 scale (1 – not a very happy person, 7 – a very happy person). A mean score is calculated as the overall score.
  - **The Oxford Happiness Questionnaire:** This measure (Hills & Argyle, 2002) includes 29 items, scored on a 1–6 Likert agreement scale. Items include: "I feel that life is very rewarding". An average score is calculated to reflect overall happiness.
- **Other measures:**
  - **Experience Sampling Methodology (ESM):** An alternative method that circumvents the typical drawbacks of questionnaires is ESM (Pavot, 2018). It prompts participants at random times to record their thoughts and emotions on a mobile device, enabling researchers to calculate an average happiness score for each person and to analyse changes across time, locations and circumstances.
  - **Other methods:** There are other means to measure happiness, including interviews, physiological measures (such as brain activity and hormone levels) and ratings of emotional experiences reflected in facial expressions (Diener et al., 2018).

All the measures have been widely used and demonstrate robust psychometric properties (Pavot, 2018).

- **Combined life satisfaction measures:**
  - **The Australian Unity (2021) Wellbeing Index** elicits people's satisfaction in seven life domains: health, relationships, standard of living, achievements, community connectedness, personal safety and future security (which refers to job, health, the environment and other factors).

Example item includes: "How satisfied are you with your standard of living"? Each question is answered on a 0–10 satisfaction scale. Scores are then combined across the domains to yield an overall score, which is adjusted to range between 0 and 100.

Conclusion

Happiness is a complex and multifaceted construct that continues to be a central focus of academic inquiry, public policy and personal aspiration. While the political valorisation of happiness has contributed to its widespread societal prominence, it has also been subject to critique for fostering unrealistic expectations and cultural preoccupations. Positive Psychology has been instrumental in advancing the scientific study of happiness, yet debates persist regarding its conceptual clarity and measurement validity. The field has largely converged on the notion that happiness and subjective wellbeing are synonymous terms, with subjective wellbeing encompassing cognitive evaluations of one's contentment with life and emotional experiences. However, this dual-component model presents methodological limitations, especially when life satisfaction and affect are treated interchangeably or used as standalone indicators of happiness.

The tension between bottom-up and top-down theories underscores the interplay between external life circumstances and internal psychological dispositions, with scholars increasingly acknowledging the bidirectional nature of this relationship. Ultimately, advancing our understanding of happiness demands an integrative approach, one that accounts not only for individual psychology but also for the broader social, cultural and structural forces that shape human wellbeing.

Limitations and Critique

Over the years, significant criticism has been directed at the competing and often ambiguous concepts of happiness and wellbeing and their corresponding measures.

Wellbeing

- **Confusing terminology:** A noteworthy weakness and a major source of confusion lie in the numerous terms used to describe wellbeing. Key terms such as quality of life, health and wellness are frequently used interchangeably (Lomas et al., 2024). Furthermore, in much of the research, terms that represent components of wellbeing, including subjective wellbeing, emotional wellbeing, happiness, utility, welfare and life satisfaction, are often conflated with wellbeing (Pincus, 2023; Kimball & Willis, 2023). Additional muddle emerges from the multiple terms that denote high or low levels of wellbeing, including optimal wellbeing, flourishing, thriving and on the low side, distress, suffering, struggling and ailing, which are often indistinct (Lomas et al., 2024).

These terminological ambiguities extend into the domains of wellbeing, where concepts such as physical, occupational, social, psychological and financial wellbeing also encounter the use of multiple synonymous terms and vague definitions and interpretations.

- **Health and wellbeing:** Lomas et al. (2024) differentiated between the concepts of health and wellbeing, and defined health as "the quality of one's personal objective state" (p. 8). The authors contended that the primary difference between health and wellbeing lies in their assessment methods: health is evaluated objectively, while wellbeing is assessed subjectively. However, this distinction does not align well with some key measures of overall wellbeing used in national or other large-scale surveys, many of which include objective measures such as income or education within their definitions and measures of wellbeing.
- **Flourishing and thriving:** These concepts are often used interchangeably, hence generating confusion. VanderWeele and Lomas (2023) differentiated between the two by defining flourishing as a high state of wellbeing that emerges under favourable circumstances, whereas thriving refers to achieving a comparable state of wellbeing attained despite facing challenging or inhospitable contexts.
- **Multiple definitions:** Another point that has attracted extensive critique is the lack of an agreed-upon definition of wellbeing. Lomas et al. (2024) noted that despite significant efforts, the question of how wellbeing should be defined remains largely unresolved, which has led to "blurred and overly broad definitions of wellbeing" (Forgeard et al., 2011, p. 81). Pollard and Lee (2003, p. 60) noted that wellbeing is "a complex, multi-faceted construct that has continued to elude researchers' attempts to define and measure". A similar critique is present in most theoretical papers on wellbeing, though it is seldom acknowledged in empirical research.
- **The components of wellbeing:** Pincus (2023) analysed the diverse wellbeing life domains included in 40 leading wellbeing surveys and found that the number of domains ranged from 4 to 17. Most wellbeing frameworks incorporate physical, social and mental dimensions. In addition, about 60% of wellbeing measures include spiritual, intellectual, occupational, financial and environmental dimensions. Only a few frameworks account for other dimensions such as growth, creativity, identity and autonomy. These discrepancies in the dimensions included in the conceptualisations and measures of overall wellbeing undermine the ability to compare research findings.
- **Independent wellbeing domains:** Certain domains of wellbeing have been studied independently from their overarching concept, evolving into distinct research fields with specific measurement tools. The most

significantly developed domains include physical wellbeing (Burke et al., 2022), psychological wellbeing (Ryff, 2014), work wellbeing (Donaldson et al., 2022) and financial wellbeing (Riitsalu et al., 2023). However, researchers do not always make a clear distinction as to which domain of wellbeing is examined and measured, and the term overall wellbeing is often confused, particularly with mental wellbeing.

- **Multiple incompatible measures:** The measures mentioned in this chapter are chosen from a wide range of instruments available for assessing overall wellbeing. This diversity of questionnaires complicates the comparison and interpretation of research findings across studies, thereby hindering the development of robust theories. Despite their limitations, these measures mark a significant shift in the assessment of wellbeing. Traditionally, wellbeing was conceptualised in terms of the absence of illness – an approach rooted in the pathogenetic model. By contrast, the more recent measures discussed here reflect a salutogenetic approach, emphasising the positive aspects of wellbeing.
- **WEIRD measures:** Most of the existing wellbeing scales are in English and have been tested predominantly in Western countries (Henrich et al., 2010), and hence a common critique of these inventories is that they may not translate well across different cultures (Lomas et al., 2024).
- **Multidisciplinary interest with scarce collaboration:** Although there has been a surge of publications on wellbeing across multiple disciplines, there appears to be minimal cross-disciplinary cooperation or discussion. Researchers are therefore encouraged to engage in such dialogues to reach a consensus on key issues (such as the terminology used for wellbeing and its sub-domains) and help advance the field.

Happiness

- **Multiple terms:** One of the main critiques surrounding the topic of happiness is the plethora of terms used to describe it. In Psychology, happiness is often used interchangeably with subjective wellbeing, hedonia and hedonic wellbeing (Hart, 2020), and in economics these terms are often used synonymously with utility and welfare (Ng, 2003). Additionally, happiness is frequently conflated with broader concepts such as overall wellbeing, flourishing and mental wellbeing, as well as with its components: satisfaction with life, life evaluation and emotional or affective wellbeing (Lomas et al., 2024). The use of multiple terms results in confusion, which extends to the measurement of happiness.

  It is noteworthy that in Economics, there has been a shift away from using the terms utility and welfare, opting instead for terms like subjective wellbeing or satisfaction with life. This change aligns with the interdisciplinary terminology that is beginning to emerge in the field. Researchers are therefore urged to use terminology that reflects the specific measures employed in their research.

- **incompatible measures:** Similar to the measures of wellbeing, numerous measures have been developed over the years to measure happiness. This hampers the ability to compare results across studies.
- **The components of subjective wellbeing:** Combining satisfaction with life and a person's emotional experience into a single composite scale has proven challenging. As a result, researchers often take shortcuts, using satisfaction with life or emotion measures as proxies for happiness. However, the correlation between the affective and evaluative measures of subjective wellbeing across the globe seems to vary (Berlin & Connolly, 2019) typically averaging around r = .50 (Koots-Ausmees et al., 2013). This suggests that the two components are distinct and that people may report high daily happiness while having low life evaluations. For example, Knabe et al. (2010) found that while unemployed individuals are much less satisfied with their lives than the employed, there are no differences between the two groups regarding daily positive and negative emotions. As the authors described, the unemployed are "dissatisfied with life, but having a good day". This suggests that using only one of the components to represent happiness may not always be accurate or relevant.

These points indicate that both wellbeing and happiness remain conceptually important yet unstable constructs, marked by terminological confusion, overlapping definitions, divergent components and incompatible measures. Such ambiguity shapes how these constructs are operationalised, compared and interpreted across studies, and therefore limits theoretical coherence and cumulative knowledge building. The proliferation of Western measures and the relative lack of cross-disciplinary dialogue further intensifies these problems. Moving the field forward requires greater conceptual precision, clearer differentiation between overarching constructs and their components or domains, more culturally sensitive and theoretically grounded measures and stronger interdisciplinary collaboration to develop a more coherent science of wellbeing and happiness.

Conclusion

This chapter established the conceptual foundations for understanding financial wellbeing by situating it within the broader framework of overall wellbeing and its key constituent – happiness. Wellbeing is widely regarded as the experience of a "life well lived", which incorporates the affective dimension of feeling good (hedonia) and the functional dimension of functioning well (eudaimonia). Rather than opposing forces, these dimensions are mutually reinforcing and form the basis of a dynamic, context-sensitive model of human flourishing.

As an umbrella term, overall wellbeing encompasses a wide range of life domains, including physical health, social relationships, work and financial wellbeing.

Within this broader framework, happiness is conceptualised as a subset of wellbeing. It comprises a cognitive element – life satisfaction and an emotional component, reflected in the balance of positive and negative affect.

Hart (2020) used an iceberg metaphor to describe overall wellbeing, arguing that the hedonic (feel-good) facets of wellbeing are often more visible and can offer an indication of a person's eudaimonic (function-well) wellbeing elements. However, happiness does not offer a complete picture of what lies below the waterline, and thus the two concepts should be treated as distinct components of wellbeing.

The diversity of tools used to measure both happiness and overall wellbeing underscores the complexity of these constructs, highlighting their nuanced nature, which is difficult to capture with a single metric. The limitations and critiques reviewed in this chapter highlight the conceptual ambiguity, terminological inconsistency and measurement challenges that permeate both wellbeing and happiness research. Yet, these critiques do not undermine the importance of these constructs; rather, they call for greater definitional clarity and methodological precision.

As we turn to the exploration of financial wellbeing, it becomes essential to carry forward both the conceptual insights and critical perspectives outlined in this chapter. Doing so will allow for a more integrated and nuanced exploration of financial wellbeing, its antecedents and its implications for human flourishing.

5 Financial Wellbeing

Financial wellbeing is a vital component of human life, reflecting the ambition to attain financial success, security and stability. The quest for economic affluence corresponds with the wider goal of leading "a good life", where the evolution of our lives aligns with our aspirations. Central to our pursuit of financial wellbeing is an innate human desire for financial abundance. This ingrained yearning extends beyond the pursuit of financial resources. It reflects our need for safety and the will to provide for our loved ones, shape our destinies, engage confidently with our environment and enjoy the liberties afforded by financial resources.

This chapter delves into the central theme of the book: financial wellbeing. It begins by providing a definition of financial wellbeing and then explores its essential elements, criteria and measures. Next, the chapter reviews concepts that are linked to and often used as synonymous terms for financial wellbeing, including financial satisfaction, resilience, stress and vulnerability.

CONCEPTUALISING FINANCIAL WELLBEING

Financial wellbeing forms a crucial part of overall wellbeing, complementing other dimensions of wellbeing such as physical, occupational, social and psychological wellbeing. Similar to overall wellbeing, the concept of financial wellbeing has been explored across multiple disciplines, including Economics, Marketing, Financial Planning, Economic Psychology and Consumer Psychology. Due to the multi-disciplinary academic interest, multiple terms, definitions, theoretical models and scales have been devised, but a consensus around them has remained elusive. With these conceptual discrepancies in mind, the review that follows delineates the key conceptualisations applied in this field, with the aim of highlighting potential areas of integration and concurrence.

Approaches to Financial Wellbeing

The various descriptions and measures of financial wellbeing can be categorised into three discrete groups based on their approach (Bruggen et al., 2017):

DOI: 10.4324/9781003415176-5

- **The objective approach:** Early research predominantly relied on objective factors, such as income, wealth, expenditure or liabilities, to assess a person, a household or an organisation's financial wellbeing.
- **The subjective approach:** A more recent approach emphasises the subjective nature of financial wellbeing and examines people's perceptions of and responses to their financial situations, assessing aspects such as financial satisfaction, confidence, sense of control or worry.
- **The combined approach:** A third approach conceptualises financial wellbeing as a synthesis of both objective and subjective elements.

Financial Wellbeing: Competing Definitions

According to the Consumer Financial Protection Bureau (CFPB, 2017, p. 13) often cited definition, **financial wellbeing** is "a state of being wherein a person can fully meet current and ongoing financial obligations, can feel secure in their financial future, and is able to make choices that allow them to enjoy life".

This conceptualisation combines several objective dimensions (such as having savings, insurance and pension plans, being able to meet financial obligations and absorb financial shocks), together with a person's subjective assessment of their financial situation (financial comfort, autonomy, security, stress, scarcity and capacity to enjoy life). It is therefore seen as a means to appraise whether a person or a household is able to lead an assured and comfortable life, with their current resources and in the future, which denotes the dynamic nature of financial wellbeing.

Taking a different approach, Salignac et al. (2020) applied the principles of wellbeing, as outlined in Positive Psychology (see Chapter 4), to develop a conceptual framework for financial wellbeing. This approach draws a distinction between hedonic (feeling good) and eudaimonic (functioning well) dimensions, and perceives wellbeing (overall or within each life domain) as an amalgamation of both. Accordingly, the authors defined financial wellbeing as "how happy people are with their current financial situation, and their ability to function economically" (p. 1583).

Drawing on the definition of wellbeing more broadly (see Chater 4), which is aligned with Salignac et al.'s (2020) conception, financial wellbeing can be understood as a continuum denoting a person's subjective assessment as to the degree to which they have attained a state of quality in the financial domain (Lomas et al., 2024).

Financial flourishing can be described as a positive state of financial wellbeing.

It is worth noting that financial wellbeing remains a concept marked by substantial definitional plurality, with authors identifying multiple definitions and noting the lack of consensus around them (see critique section below). This lack of agreement partly reflects the different approaches outlined above, with some definitions privileging objective financial conditions, others subjective evaluations and others integrating both. The CFPB's (2017) combines objective and subjective dimensions, whereas Salignac et al.'s (2020) conceptualisation is explicitly subjective. Taken together, these variations suggest that financial wellbeing is, at this point in time, an evolving concept whose definition depends on the theoretical lens through which it is approached.

Components of Financial Wellbeing

A healthy level of financial wellbeing is characterised by an individual's or a household's ability to meet certain markers (Fan & Henager, 2022; Bruggen et al., 2017; Riitsalu et al., 2023; Salignac et al., 2020; Castro-González et al., 2020; Kempson et al., 2017; Zyphur et al., 2015; CFPB, 2015a). These are often described in the literature as criteria or components of financial wellbeing, and entail mostly subjective dimensions:

- Having control over personal finances.
- Being able to manage one's finances effectively.
- Comfortably meeting financial commitments and needs.
- Being able to make choices that allow enjoyment in life.
- Progress is made towards achieving future financial goals.
- Having the capacity to sustain current and anticipated living standards.
- The ability to meet unexpected future expenses and weather financial shocks.
- Being satisfied with their financial situation.
- Experiencing financial security.
- Rarely experiencing negative emotional states such as financial stress, worry or anxiety.

These criteria frame financial wellbeing as a multifaceted construct that includes autonomy, security, control and comfort (Bruggen et al., 2017; CFPB, 2015a) and thus extends beyond the absence of financial hardship or distress. This suggests that avoiding hardship is insufficient to produce a positive state of financial wellbeing.

It is also crucial to distinguish between financial resources, such as income and wealth, and financial wellbeing. While financial wellbeing is influenced by income and monetary assets, and having sufficient resources contributes to financial satisfaction, security and reduced stress (Collins & Urban, 2021; Netemeyer et al., 2018) the concept of financial wellbeing is broader than income and wealth, and encompasses subjective evaluations, as Bruggen et al. (2017, p. 230) noted: "individuals may experience high or low financial wellbeing regardless of their objective financial position".

Measures of Financial Wellbeing

Research on financial wellbeing largely employs quantitative methodologies, incorporating varied scales that capture the construct or explore specific facets of it. The following are examples of the more commonly used scales.

- **The Consumer Financial Protection Bureau (CFPB, 2015b) Financial Wellbeing Scale** features ten items that prompt individuals to evaluate the applicability of certain statements to themselves or their circumstances. These are scored on a 0–4 Likert agreement scale and summed up to obtain an overall score. Items are mainly subjective and include people's assessment of their capacity to handle unexpected expenses, feeling secure regarding the future, experiencing a sense of scarcity, being able to enjoy life, having financial concerns, having money left at the end of the month, being behind with payments and having a sense that life is controlled by their financial situation.
- **The InCharge Financial Distress/Financial Wellbeing Scale** (Prawitz et al., 2006) includes eight items that assess respondents' financial stress levels, financial satisfaction, sense of comfort regarding one's financial situation, financial worry, capacity to cover emergency expenses, inability to afford everyday expenses and living paycheque to paycheque. Items are subjective, scored on a 1–10 Likert agreement scale and summed up to derive an overall score.
- **The Financial Wellbeing Questionnaire** (Netemeyer et al., 2018) includes two subjective dimensions:
  - The stress subscale includes five items that examine a person's sense of deprivation, being behind with one's finances, feeling that life is controlled by one's financial situation, experiencing significant financial hindrances and reporting on an inability to enjoy life.
  - The financial security scale entails five items that examine confidence in achieving financial goals, efforts to achieve financial security, having enough savings to cater for future needs, becoming financially secure and confidence that the future is protected financially.

Items on both subscales are scored on a 1–5 Likert agreement scale, and each subscale is summed separately.

- **The Financial Wellbeing Questionnaire** is often used in the banking industry (Comerton-Forde et al., 2022) and includes two subscales:
  - The subjective measure included ten items, each scored on a 0–4 Likert agreement scale. Example item includes: "I feel on top of my day to day finances".
  - The objective measure included five items, each scored on a 0–4 Likert frequency scale. Items include: "Payment problems in last year".

Each subscale is scored independently by summing its respective items.

- **The Financial Strain Questionnaire,** developed by Aldana and Liljenquist (1998), combines objective and subjective measures. It comprises 18 items and 5 subscales:
  - **Education:** Understanding interest paid on loans or other debts and feeling informed and knowledgeable.
  - **Relationships:** Money disagreements, arguing about money and money problems affecting relationships.
  - **Physical health:** Experiencing sleep problems, headaches, muscle pain or digestive problems due to money issues.
  - **Credit card usage:** Use of a credit card for everyday purchases and accumulating debt.
  - **The ability to meet financial obligations:** Paying bills on time and difficulty in paying bills.

Items are scored on a 1–5 Likert frequency scale, and a mean is calculated for each subscale.

Financial Wellbeing around the Globe

Recent attempts to assess the percentage of people (or households) with healthy levels of financial wellbeing found significant differences between studies and countries. A large-scale UK study (Evans et al., 2024) found that 61% of households were showing reasonable to high financial wellbeing, demonstrating a decrease of 11% from 2020. In Ireland, 39% reported positive financial wellbeing (Statista, 2024). A survey by Fidelity (2024) reported that in Japan, 62% of participants ranked their financial wellbeing as good; in Germany – 64%; in Hong Kong – 65%; in Canada – 69%; and in China – 88%. A recent report from the FRS (2023) in the US found that 73% of people self-rated their financial wellbeing as satisfactory and above. However, it is noteworthy that each survey used different measures, which makes the comparison challenging.

Conclusion

This section has outlined the conceptual foundations of financial wellbeing, emphasising its central role in shaping overall wellbeing and quality of life. It has shown that financial wellbeing is a multidimensional construct, encompassing both objective indicators and subjective perceptions. Despite the diversity of definitions and measurement tools across disciplines, a unifying theme emerges: financial wellbeing extends beyond material sufficiency to reflect a broader sense of control, confidence and financial resilience. This conceptual breadth highlights the importance of integrating multiple perspectives to better understand and support individuals. financial lives.

INTERSECTING CONCEPTS

Researchers have noted that a variety of concepts partially intersect with sound levels of financial wellbeing, such as financial resilience, security and satisfaction. However, in much of the literature, their areas of overlap with and distinction from financial wellbeing are not clarified. Similarly, concepts that indicate poor financial wellbeing, such as financial fragility, hardship, vulnerability, stress and anxiety, are rarely clarified and distinguished from low levels of financial wellbeing. The following brief review seeks to describe and clarify the key concepts intersecting with financial wellbeing, aiming to highlight potential areas of integration and correspondence.

Financial Stress

Financial stress is one of the most prevalent and enduring types of stress. According to a recent FCA (2023) survey, 54% of UK adults experience financial stress. In the US, the rate of financial distress is similarly high, with 47% of US adults reporting that money has a negative impact on their mental health (Bankrate, 2024).

> Building on the well-established Transactional Model of Stress and Coping (Lazarus & Folkman, 1984), Friedline et al. (2021) defined **financial stress** as a psychological, physiological and behavioural reactions that arise when individuals assess that they are unable to meet their financial obligations, afford essential life necessities or have sufficient funds to make ends meet.

This definition suggests the concept of stress is fundamentally subjective: two people experiencing the same financial circumstances may evaluate their situations differently, leading to varying levels of stress and distinct psychological, physiological and behavioural responses. It also conceptualises financial stress as a sequence of reactions stemming from the interaction between an individual and their financial environment. Stress arises when the financial demands are perceived as exceeding the individual's capacity to meet them. Therefore, financial stress stems from an imbalance between one's resources and their financial needs or obligations (Friedline et al., 2021).

Importantly, stress is not only a consequence of financial hardship, but also a factor that can further worsen a person's financial situation (Haushofer & Salicath, 2023). Chronic financial stress can impair physical and mental health, coping mechanisms and cognitive resources, thereby hampering a person's capacity to function effectively in the financial domain, hence perpetuating a vicious cycle that is difficult to break.

Measuring Financial Stress

The one-item stress measure: A single item is often used to measure financial stress: "How stressed do you feel about your current financial situation?" Answers range between 1 and 10 on a Likert severity scale (Britt et al., 2016).

As previously mentioned, some research on financial wellbeing considers financial stress as an indicator of poor financial wellbeing, and hence, the absence of stress is seen as a sign of healthy financial wellbeing (Prawitz et al., 2006; Netemeyer et al., 2018). However, equating financial wellbeing solely with the absence of financial stress fails to capture the complexity of financial wellbeing and the various components that it encompasses.

Financial Anxiety and Worry

Financial anxiety and worry are negative thoughts and emotions triggered by one's financial situation. They are central components of financial wellbeing as they capture its emotional aspect. Both financial worry and anxiety manifest as concerns about managing day-to-day expenses, meeting current financial obligations, apprehension about future financial stability and the potential impact of financial decisions or unexpected expenses. Individuals experiencing financial worry and anxiety frequently feel burdened by their financial responsibilities and insecure about their financial future (Grable et al., 2015).

Financial anxiety is defined as a negative emotional response characterised by apprehension, agitation, fear or panic related to one's financial situation (Grable et al., 2015). The emotional response is often accompanied by cognitive reactions (such as fearful or catastrophising thoughts) and physical responses (such as higher blood pressure and faster heartbeat).

Financial worry involves persistent and often obsessive thoughts about financial matters (Magwegwe et al., 2023), which can produce corresponding emotional and physiological reactions.

Similar to financial stress, when financial anxiety or worry is experienced as excessive, it can severely interfere with an individual's daily functioning, as it can impair cognitive function, decrease productivity and deteriorate physical health, thus perpetuating a cycle of financial inactivity and instability (Grable et al., 2015; Magwegwe et al., 2023).

A critique that can be levelled at both concepts is that the distinction between them is unclear and requires some nuanced conceptual and methodological work to untie them.

Financial Anxiety and Worry Measures

- **Financial anxiety measure:** Grable et al. (2015) utilised a single item to measure financial anxiety, asking participants to rate their anxiety about their current financial situation on a 1–10 severity scale. Additionally, the authors employed a 7-item scale with statements such as: "I feel anxious about my financial situation". Responses are recorded on a 1–7 frequency scale and summed up to produce an overall score.
- **Financial worry measure:** De Bruijn and Antonides (2020) developed a financial worry scale that differentiates between cognitions and emotions. The emotions subscale includes four items, such as: "I feel anxious when I think about my finances", while the cognitions subscale includes four items, such as: "I think a lot about how to solve financial problems". Items are answered on a 5-point agreement scale, and sub-scales are separately summed up.

Financial Strain and Hardship

> **Financial strain and hardship** pertain to the concrete and quantifiable challenges in fulfilling financial obligations. It involves the objective financial burdens faced by an individual or household, such as struggles to pay bills, meet loan payments or afford basic necessities (Ettman et al., 2023).

These definitions imply that financial strain and hardship are objective, synonymous terms, although semantically, hardship may indicate more grave circumstances than strain.

Measuring Financial Strain and Hardship

Measures of financial strain and hardship directly assess the nature and extent of deprivation that a person is experiencing relative to their own needs.

- **The Economic Strain Model** (Pearlin et al., 1981) is a 9-item scale that assesses a person's ability to pay for clothing, medical care, housing, food, leisure activities, transportation and furniture, difficulty paying bills and the ability to make ends meet. These are scored on a 1–4 Likert frequency scale and summed up into a total hardship score.
- **The Economic Hardship Questionnaire** (Lempers et al., 1989) includes ten items that require participants to consider their financial behaviours in the past six months. Items include behaviours that offer indications of hardship, such as cutting back on social activities and entertainment, postponing major purchases and taking on additional employment to meet expenses. These are scored on a 1–4 frequency scale and summed up to derive a total score.

Financial strain and hardship offer important indications of how deprivation translates into daily struggles. These are essential for capturing the impact of poverty and can be used for assessing the needs of households and for providing support or intervention strategies.

Financial Vulnerability and Fragility

The capacity to endure shocks like a sudden income drop, job loss or unexpected expenses is a key aspect of financial wellbeing. Financial vulnerability is frequently associated with poverty and refers to an individual's or household's inability to manage financial risks or shocks (Swain & Floro, 2007).

Financial vulnerability and fragility are defined as a household's inability to cover unexpected expenses (Anderloni et al., 2012).

A household is considered vulnerable if it cannot fund its retirement needs or repay its debts. Financial fragility is a subset of vulnerability, which focuses on households' ability to manage financial emergencies (Lusardi et al., 2011).

While vulnerability and fragility can stem from life events such as job loss, a death in the family, illness and unexpected expenses, researchers assess that a key cause in many cases is unsound or unsustainable borrowing decisions, leading households to accumulate debt that is disproportionate to their earning capacity (Anderloni et al., 2012).

Measures of Financial Vulnerability and Fragility

Various measures evaluate financial vulnerability:

- **Financial fragility:** Lusardi et al. (2011) assessed financial fragility with a single questionnaire item asking participants if they could cover a $400 emergency expense immediately, or afford a $2,000 unexpected expense within a month. Despite its simplicity, this measure has proven to be valuable and has been widely used in research.
- **Financial vulnerability:** Anderloni et al. (2012) evaluated financial vulnerability through the use of two measures: assessing debt to income ratio and gathering information on savings levels, difficulties in meeting daily expenses, the ability to handle unexpected costs and changes in households' economic situations over the past 12 months, and future expectations.

While financial vulnerability and fragility constructs and scales provide valuable insights into the objective aspects of an individual's financial circumstances, they fall short in capturing their subjective dimensions.

Financial Satisfaction

Financial satisfaction (also termed subjective financial wellbeing) is defined as an individual's level of contentment with their current financial circumstances (Fan & Henager, 2022).

The concept of financial satisfaction is often employed in research to represent the subjective, evaluative aspect of financial wellbeing. As such, it is regarded as a component of financial wellbeing, encompassing a cognitive self-assessment of an individual's financial situation. Financial satisfaction is also an aspect of overall life satisfaction, alongside other life domains such as health, work and relationships.

Assessing Financial Satisfaction

- **The single-item measure of financial satisfaction** is widely used across numerous studies. It originated from Prawitz et al.'s (2006) InCharge Financial Distress/Financial Wellbeing Scale and asks: "How satisfied are you with your financial situation"? Responses are rated on a 10-point scale.
- **The Financial Satisfaction Scale** (Archuleta et al., 2013) comprises four items assessing respondents' satisfaction across key aspects of their financial lives: the amount of money they have saved, their level of debt, their capacity to achieve long-term financial goals and their income level. Each item is rated on a 10-point satisfaction scale, and the total score is obtained by summing responses across all items.

Confusingly, however, in some studies, the term financial satisfaction is used interchangeably with financial wellbeing (Fan & Henager, 2022). Researchers have noted that there is a strong positive association between financial satisfaction and financial wellbeing (Joo & Grable, 2004; Vlaev & Elliott, 2014), which partially justifies the use of financial satisfaction as a proxy for financial wellbeing.

Financial Security

Financial security refers to the state of having stable and sufficient financial resources to meet one's needs and obligations, both in the present and the future (Lyons et al., 2018).

The concept of financial security encompasses not only the availability of financial resources but also the confidence that these resources will be adequate to sustain one's standard of living, manage unexpected expenses and achieve financial goals. Financial security includes elements such as income stability, savings and the absence of excessive debt, contributing to overall financial wellbeing and peace of mind (Lyons et al., 2018).

Measuring Financial Security

Munyon et al. (2020) developed a 5-item questionnaire for financial security. A sample item includes: "I have adequate income", and these are marked on a 7-point Likert agreement scale and summed up to derive an overall score.

The description and measure of the financial security construct reveal some overlaps with the previously reviewed concepts of strain, vulnerability and hardship.

Financial Resilience

Financial resilience is defined as patterns of positive adaptation in the face of financial adversity (Salignac et al., 2019). It refers to the capacity of individuals or households to withstand and recover from financial shocks or adversities, such as unexpected expenses, loss of income or economic downturns. It encompasses the ability to manage financial resources effectively, adapt to changing circumstances and maintain financial stability in the face of challenges.

Drawing on resilience scholarship (Lepore & Revenson, 2014), Salignac et al. (2019) identified several types of financial resilience:

- **Resistance:** This form of financial resilience occurs when individuals show minimal or no disturbance when facing financial hardship.
- **Recovery:** This type of financial resilience is exhibited by individuals who experience short-term disruption when facing financial adversity, but after a recovery period, return to their regular pre-stressor level of financial functioning.
- **Reconfiguration:** This form of resilience emerges when individuals adjust their lives and create a new normal way of financial functioning after facing adversity.
- **Succumbing:** When individuals exhibit low financial resilience, they may experience long-term financial impairments.

Resilience is heavily dependent on access to appropriate resources, often described as protective factors. From this perspective, financial resilience can be viewed as an equation where an individual's protective factors outweigh the risks posed by financial adversity (Morduch & Schneider, 2017). These resources could be financial – such as having emergency savings, diversified income sources and access to credit – but they also entail capacities, traits or other resources such as financial literacy, optimism, the capacity to manage stress and make sound financial decisions during crises and social support (Salignac et al., 2019).

Measures of Financial Resilience

- **The Financial Resilience Framework questionnaire:** This scale (Salignac et al., 2019) includes 15 items and four subscales and includes objective and subjective items:
  - **Economic resources:** This subscale assesses a household's level of savings, debt, ability to raise emergency funds, ability to meet living expenses and household income.
  - **Financial products:** This dimension evaluates an individual's capacity to access financial products and their level of need for these products, including a bank account, credit, insurance, unmet credit need and unmet insurance need.
  - **Financial knowledge and behaviour:** This subscale measures financial knowledge, confidence, advice-seeking and proactive financial decision-making.
  - **Social capital:** This component evaluates the availability of social networks, social support and community or government support.

All items are scored on a 1–4 scale, with lower scores indicating fewer resources. To calculate a composite resilience score, a mean of all items is computed.

Conclusion

The intersecting concepts reviewed in this section underscore the multidimensional nature of financial wellbeing. These concepts capture distinct but often interrelated psychological, behavioural and material dimensions of individuals' financial lives. However, despite their interconnectedness, they are frequently treated in isolation, with conceptual overlap and terminological ambiguity limiting both theoretical clarity and practical application. A more integrated understanding is needed, one that distinguishes between antecedents, components and outcomes of financial wellbeing, while accounting for both subjective and objective experiences.

Clarifying the boundaries between intersecting concepts and financial wellbeing can support more precise measurement, guide intervention design and foster theoretical advancement. Future research should aim to disentangle these constructs conceptually and empirically, building models that acknowledge their interdependence but avoid conflation. Such efforts will help advance a more holistic and nuanced account of what constitutes financial wellbeing in contemporary contexts.

Limitations and Critique

Much like the concept of wellbeing (discussed in Chapter 4), financial wellbeing and its auxiliary concepts also face similar limitations and have attracted considerable critique.

Financial Wellbeing

- **Multiple terms:** Within scholarly literature and industry publications, a variety of terms are used interchangeably. These include financial wellness, financial resilience, economic wellbeing, perceived financial wellbeing, financial satisfaction and financial health, which is the key term used in the financial industry. This terminological ambiguity has attracted significant critique, with researchers calling for clarification of these terms and for unification (Riitsalu et al., 2023).
- **Conceptual ambiguity around definitions:** There are numerous definitions of financial wellbeing in the literature, and in a recent paper, Garcia-Mata and Zeron-Felix (2022) identified 18 definitions. Riitsalu et al. (2023) noted that there is no consensus around a singular definition. Consequently, researchers exploring this topic often start by recognising the variety of definitions, and then either adopt a specific definition for their investigation or introduce a new interpretation. These conceptual disagreements influence the creation and use of measurement tools, hence generating multiple and incompatible measures. They also hamper the capacity to compare findings across studies.

- **Financial wellbeing criteria:** There is ongoing disagreement in the literature regarding the appropriate criteria by which financial wellbeing should be assessed. The ten components of financial wellbeing cited above were drawn from several papers (Fan & Henager, 2022; Bruggen et al., 2017; Riitsalu et al., 2023; Salignac et al., 2020; Castro-González et al., 2020; Kempson et al., 2017). However, each of these papers mentioned between 2 and 5 components, and none cited all ten. This suggests that there are discrepancies in the literature in the identification of the components of financial wellbeing. These inconsistencies undermine the capacity to compare the conceptualisations that exist across papers, and when embedded into the common measures of financial wellbeing, they create further difficulties.
- **The components of financial wellbeing:** The conceptualisations of financial wellbeing in the literature often include financial satisfaction, resilience, security and financial stress as fundamental components. These are often used as proxies for financial wellbeing (Garcia-Mata & Zeron-Felix, 2022; Netemeyer et al., 2018). This conflation blurs the distinction between the components of financial wellbeing and synonymous terms, leading to inconsistencies in measurement and interpretation.
- **Incompatible measures:** The questionnaires mentioned above represent a fraction of the extensive range of instruments that researchers employ to assess financial wellbeing. The diverse array of questionnaires complicates the comparison and interpretation of research findings across different studies, which in turn obstructs the development of theory.
- **Culturally biased measures:** The majority of financial wellbeing scales are in English and were developed in Western countries, and therefore, they may not be suitable for measuring financial wellbeing cross-culturally (Riitsalu et al., 2023).
- **Validity issues:** Concerns have also been raised regarding the validity of financial wellbeing questionnaires. Riitsalu et al. (2023) identified problems related to both content and construct validity:
  - Content validity issues arise when items within a scale do not accurately represent the concept being measured (Howitt & Cramer, 2020). For instance, certain scales of financial wellbeing incorporate items related to financial behaviours, therefore muddying the distinction between financial wellbeing and financial behaviours.
  - A lack of discriminant validity typically arises when there are high correlations between the scores of a given measure and those of other measures (Howitt & Cramer, 2020). For instance, if a financial wellbeing questionnaire includes questions related to financial capabilities, it may show high correlations with measures of financial capabilities, which could be attributed to the overlap of items in the questionnaires.
  - Construct validity pertains to how well a tool measures the theoretical concept it is intended to measure (Howitt & Cramer, 2020).

This implies that the components associated with financial wellbeing (such as maintaining control over finances or meeting financial obligations) should be reflected in the scales designed to measure it. However, the available scales only capture a subset of the financial wellbeing components presented earlier, with no existing scale comprehensively measuring all the components of financial wellbeing outlined by scholars.

Intersecting Concepts

- **Lack of clarity:** The review of auxiliary concepts intersecting with financial wellbeing indicates a persistent lack of clarity, with several concepts overlapping. For example, the terms financial stress, distress, hardship or strain are used in some of the literature interchangeably, while financial strain, hardship, vulnerability and fragility partially overlap both in their definitions and in their measures (French & Vigne, 2019; Frankham et al., 2020).

  This semantic ambiguity in terminology and definitions risks exposing financial wellbeing research to the jingle-jangle fallacies. Kelley (1927), who coined the term, noted that a jingle fallacy occurs when a concept fails to distinguish between different constructs, while a jangle fallacy happens when two concepts with different names refer to the same construct. To avoid these fallacies, it is necessary to clarify and unify terminology, definitions and theoretical concepts.

  Beyond the confusion that this terminological ambiguity generates, it also limits researchers' ability to search for literature, presents challenges in comparing findings and hinders the development of a coherent theoretical framework for financial wellbeing.

The limitations reviewed here suggest that financial wellbeing remains an important but still insufficiently consolidated construct. Across both financial wellbeing and its intersecting concepts, the field is marked by terminological inconsistency, definitional overlap, disputed criteria and fragmented measurement practices, all of which weaken conceptual precision and constrain cumulative knowledge development. Advancing this area of scholarship requires a more systematic effort to distinguish financial wellbeing from adjacent constructs, specify its core dimensions and develop theoretically grounded and cross-culturally robust measures. Such clarification is essential if financial wellbeing research is to provide a coherent basis for explanation, comparison and practical application.

Conclusion

This chapter introduced financial wellbeing as an essential aspect of human wellbeing.

From defining financial wellbeing and identifying its components, to measuring the construct, it's clear that financial wellbeing transcends the mere assessment of a person's wealth or financial status. The concept encapsulates a broader spectrum of experiences and sense-making processes, including financial satisfaction and stress, autonomy, security, control and comfort, and importantly, a sense of efficacy in one's capacity to function economically. Additionally, it also embeds a time horizon extending from the present to the future. These components are deeply interwoven, affecting and being affected by one another in a dynamic fashion.

The chapter also presented and critiqued the principal conceptual frameworks of financial wellbeing alongside their measures, as well as other concepts that intersect with financial wellbeing, shedding light on some of the methodological issues that currently impede its progress.

As the field continues to evolve, it holds the promise of enriching our theoretical understanding as well as informing applied practices, interventions and policies that can enhance our financial wellbeing and, by extension, our quality of life. The journey ahead, filled with challenges and opportunities, invites a collaborative interdisciplinary effort to untangle the conceptual and measurement complexities of financial wellbeing and leverage its potential for fostering healthier, more fulfilling lives.

6 Models of Financial Wellbeing

The previous chapter defined financial wellbeing and outlined its various measures, setting the stage for an exploration of the determinants and upshots of financial wellbeing. This chapter delves into pivotal models that provide a framework for understanding the key predictors of financial wellbeing and its outcomes. These models offer diverse perspectives and highlight different aspects of the financial wellbeing construct, paving the way for a more nuanced analysis in the subsequent chapters.

It is worth noting that several scholars presented empirical models that summarise their research findings and chart the array of factors that predict financial wellbeing that they have focused on in their work (see, for example, Comerton-Forde et al., 2022; Salignac et al., 2020; Iramani & Lutfi, 2021; Gutter & Copur, 2011; Shim et al., 2009; Fan & Henager, 2022 and others). Among the numerous models available in the literature, the models reviewed below stand out, as they are either theoretically grounded or draw on reviews of the extant literature to illustrate the key drivers of financial wellbeing found across studies.

FINANCIAL WELLBEING: ITS DETERMINANTS AND UPSHOTS

Bruggen et al. (2017) developed a comprehensive conceptual model that elucidates both the determinants and outcomes of financial wellbeing (depicted in Figure 6.1).

The model indicates that there are four key drivers of financial wellbeing:

- **Financial behaviours:** Central to this model are financial behaviours. The authors argued that financial behaviours are pivotal, directly influencing financial wellbeing and stressed the importance of engaging with positive financial behaviours, alongside restraining detrimental ones.
- **Economic interventions:** The model incorporates individual financial interventions such as financial education, counselling, advice and planning, alongside macro-level interventions such as policy changes, nudging and structural changes. These interventions are seen as mechanisms that can positively alter financial behaviours. Additionally, these

DOI: 10.4324/9781003415176-6

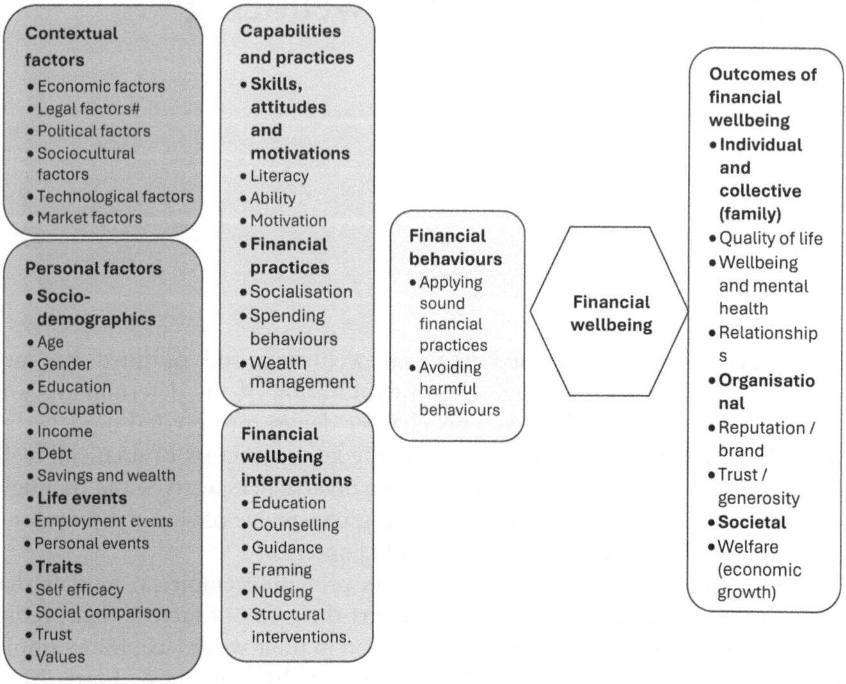

Figure 6.1 Financial wellbeing.

Adapted from Bruggen et al. (2017, p. 231)

interventions have the capacity to mitigate the effects of personal and contextual factors on financial behaviours.

- **Personal factors:** These refer to sociodemographic background, personality traits, financial literacy, skills and attitudes, financial practices and life events (such as employment or family events).
- **Contextual factors:** The contextual factors in the model primarily relate to macro-level elements, such as a country's economic development, growth rates, employment levels, legal considerations, monetary and social policies.
- **The outcomes of financial wellbeing:** The upshots of financial wellbeing included in the model pertain to several levels: individual and household level, communal, organisational and national.

When the model was first introduced, it was largely theoretical, though currently there is empirical support for most (but not all) aspects of the model. Crucially, the model effectively illustrates that certain factors directly influence financial wellbeing (particularly behaviours), whereas others have both a direct and an indirect impact. For example, skills impinge on financial wellbeing directly by contributing to a person's sense of mastery, but they also affect financial wellbeing indirectly by invoking certain behaviours.

Importantly, Bruggen et al.'s (2017) model is the only model that acknowledges the role of interventions and policies in promoting financial wellbeing. However, a critique of the model is that it does not address financial decision-making explicitly, which is a central factor in determining financial wellbeing. Additionally, there is a noticeable overlap between financial behaviours and financial practices, both of which appear to encompass similar actions. Moreover, while the model includes employment, it fails to consider other pathways to earning (such as generating income from investments or royalties). Finally, the model does not offer a compatible measure.

AN ECOLOGICAL LIFE COURSE MODEL OF FINANCIAL WELLBEING

Another model proposed by Salignac et al. (2020) adopts an ecological life-course perspective to explore the drivers of financial wellbeing. It draws on Bronfenbrenner's (2005) bioecological model and emphasises that the financial wellbeing of an individual cannot be understood without examining their environment. It therefore contextualises financial wellbeing within broad relational, social, structural and temporal dynamics.

The key aspects of the model include the following:

- **The life-course approach:** Taking a life-course perspective enables the exploration of how different life stages and events affect financial wellbeing over time. The model posits that the dimensions of financial wellbeing evolve throughout an individual's life in response to changing life stages and significant events.
- **The ecological aspect:** The key argument of the model is that financial wellbeing is influenced by the interactions between the individual and their environment, which includes personal, household, community and societal levels.
- **Individual factors:** At the personal level, factors such as financial skills, behaviours, employment, health, gender and education, alongside financial knowledge, attitudes, choice, control and feeling financially secure are identified within the model as crucial determinants of financial wellbeing. Behaviours include setting and pursuing goals, saving, investing and insuring. These factors interact with broader household and community contexts.
- **Household influences:** The next layer in the ecological system includes family and associated responsibilities, as well as parental influences and couple dynamics as key factors that impinge on financial wellbeing.
- **Community influences:** The following layer in the model includes local influences such as housing affordability and the local job market, highlighting their impact on the financial wellbeing of individuals and households.

- **Macro influences:** The external layer in the eco-system includes government policies, financial products and services and, importantly, global and national markets and events, which can significantly impinge on a person's financial resources and wellbeing.

The Bioecological Model of Human Development

Bronfenbrenner's (2005) Bioecological Model of Human Development is a seminal work that presents a framework for understanding human development within the context of various environmental systems.

Key Components

- **Microsystem:** The innermost layer includes the immediate environments that an individual interacts with, such as family, school and peer groups.
- **Mesosystem:** This layer encompasses the interconnections between the microsystems, such as the relationship between a child's home and school. It represents how these environments interact.
- **Exosystem: This layer involves the broader social systems that affect human development, such as parental workplaces, health services and extended family networks.**
- **Macrosystem: This layer comprises cultural values, laws, customs and resources. It influences all other systems and reflects the broader societal context in which the individual lives.**
- **Chronosystem: This aspect includes the dimension of time, emphasising how life transitions and historical events impact an individual's development over their lifespan.**
- **Ecological transitions:** Bronfenbrenner included ecological transitions in the model, which occur when an individual's position within their ecological environment changes as a result of life events, such as starting school, entering puberty or moving to a new city. These transitions can significantly impact development by altering the dynamics within and between the different systems.

Bronfenbrenner's ecological model has profound implications for research and practice in Developmental Psychology. It highlights the necessity of considering multiple environmental layers and suggests that interventions aimed at improving developmental outcomes should address not only the individual but also their broader environmental contexts.

To conclude, this model is grounded in Bronfenbrenner's (2005) Bioecological Model and offers substantial insights. It underscores a crucial point: the various economic contexts in which individuals operate can profoundly affect their financial resources and wellbeing. However, it also acknowledges the importance of individual agency and the capacity to navigate one's economic terrain, even in the face of considerable contextual challenges.

A key critique of the model is that it emerged from the findings of a qualitative study that involved limited data, and as such, it cannot demonstrate associations, mediators, moderators or causality. Additionally, it is unable to assess the degree of interaction between the two main intersecting factors: life span features and ecological aspects. Lastly, the model does not offer an associated measure and does not consider the downstream effects of financial wellbeing.

A SYSTEMS MODEL OF FINANCIAL WELLBEING

Brown et al. (2024) applied a systems approach to develop a theoretical model of financial wellbeing that captures the complexity of interacting factors across individual, organisational and societal levels. Their rationale stems from the observation that traditional approaches to financial wellbeing have focused disproportionately on individual-level variables, such as financial capability, while neglecting the broader social, economic and institutional systems that shape individuals' financial lives. Such reductionist perspectives often result in interventions that target symptoms rather than root causes and fail to account for the differential impacts of contexts across population groups. By contrast, a systems approach focuses on interdependency, feedback loops and contextual variability, offering a more holistic and policy-relevant framework for addressing financial wellbeing.

The components of the model include the following:

- **Micro-level drivers:** These refer to individual and household characteristics that influence how people experience and manage their financial lives. These include demographic factors such as income, age, education and employment, as well as financial capability, understood as the knowledge, skills and confidence required to make sound financial decisions. While these drivers are often the focus of policy and interventions, the model emphasises that they are shaped by, and responsive to, broader system-level conditions.
- **Meso-level drivers:** These encompass organisational and community-level influences, such as the policies and practices of banks and other financial services, employers and local support providers. Meso-level institutions affect access to employment, financial products and services that can support or hinder financial wellbeing. For example, banks' lending practices can significantly shape household financial trajectories.
- **Macro-level drivers:** These include structural and systemic forces such as economic systems, public policy, legal frameworks, social norms and

major events. Macro-level drivers influence financial wellbeing through both direct and indirect pathways. For instance, tax policies can dramatically shift household financial circumstances. Social structures, such as class, race and gender, also play a critical role, often reinforcing inequalities in financial opportunities and outcomes.

- **Interdependencies and feedback loops:** The model emphasises that these levels are interdependent. Macro- and meso-level factors primarily influence financial wellbeing through their effects on micro-level variables. However, these effects are moderated by individuals' social positions and lived contexts, meaning that identical interventions may produce divergent outcomes depending on who is affected. The model also incorporates feedback mechanisms, recognising that individuals may, to varying degrees, influence the organisations and structures around them, albeit unevenly due to disparities in power and access.

The model provides a comprehensive framework for understanding financial wellbeing, offering policymakers a valuable tool for designing interventions that go beyond treating symptoms, enabling them to address underlying causes embedded in broader systems.

A Systems Approach

A systems approach is a holistic mode of inquiry that seeks to understand the interrelationships and dynamics within complex systems, rather than analysing components in isolation (Monat & Gannon, 2015). It is rooted in General Systems Theory (Meadows, 2008) and provides a framework for examining how system components interact, evolve over time and give rise to patterns of behaviour. Unlike reductionist approaches that deconstruct phenomena into discrete elements, systems thinking emphasises synthesis, feedback loops, non-linearity and emergent properties that arise from the interplay between parts within a system. This makes it particularly suitable for addressing multifaceted challenges in domains such as socio-economic policy, environmental management and organisational strategy.

As a perspective, systems thinking involves seeing wholes rather than parts, focusing on relationships over components and considering temporal dynamics. Importantly, the approach acknowledges the phenomenon of emergence – where particular properties are a consequence of the relationships among system components (Monat & Gannon, 2015). Thus, a systems approach not only enhances explanatory power but also supports more adaptive, sustainable and informed decision-making in complex contexts.

Brown et al.'s (2024) model offers a valuable theoretical contribution by proposing a systems-informed model of financial wellbeing that moves beyond individual-level explanations to consider the dynamic interplay of micro-, meso- and macro-level drivers. The model's strengths lie in its conceptual richness, its grounding in systems theory and its potential to inform more holistic and equitable social policy. However, the model also has notable limitations, including the absence of measures, lack of empirical validation, limited operational guidance for policymakers, lack of attention to the outcomes of financial wellbeing and a strong reliance on the Australian context, which may constrain its international applicability.

MAPPING THE PREDICTORS OF FINANCIAL WELLBEING

Mahendru et al. (2022) drew on an extensive literature review and mapping exercise to develop a model which summarises the predictors of financial wellbeing, highlighting the interactions between these drivers.

The model suggests that any analysis of financial wellbeing requires taking into account simultaneously several factors and highlighting mediators and moderators. These factors include the following: the sociopolitical and economic environment within which people operate, objective factors (income and wealth, employment, financial obligations and expenses), subjective factors (financial socialisation, financial satisfaction, financial stress and happiness), financial knowledge and skills, personality (particularly emptional stability and conscientiousness) and financial behaviours. The model indicates that financial behaviours are the strongest predictors of financial wellbeing, but these behaviours are influenced by all other factors. These behaviours include saving, spending, investing, and debt management.

The model stands out for its thoroughness in identifying the numerous factors that directly and indirectly influence financial wellbeing, along with the primary mediators highlighted in scholarly research. It also offers an extensive analysis of the policy implications of these findings. Importantly, it is unique in explicitly addressing various earning behaviours beyond traditional employment.

However, it does not incorporate financial decisions, interventions or the outcomes of financial wellbeing. Additionally, it shares with Bruggen et al.'s (2017) model the issue of overlapping categories. For instance, the objective factors category includes debts, expenditures, credit use and spending patterns, which can also be considered behaviours and are listed in the behaviour category.

Model components	
Socio political and economic environment • Economic environment. • Demographic environment. • Social environment. • Political environment.	
Objective factors • Income and assets. • Employment. • Debts and expenditures.	**Subjective factors** • Financial satisfaction and strain. • Financial socialisation. • Subjective wellbeing.
Financial knowledge and skills • Financial literacy. • Financial skills. • Staying informed. • Economic environment.	
Personality • Engagement and exploration. • Emotional stability. • Conscientiousness.	
Financial behaviours • Saving behaviours. • Spending behaviours. • Investment behaviours. • Credit management behaviours	
Financial wellbeing Source: Adapted from Mahendru et al. (2022, p. 430).	

Figure 6.2 Financial wellbeing.

Adapted from Mahendru et al. (2022, p. 430)

Conclusion

The models reviewed in this section present a complex view of the drivers and upshots of financial wellbeing. All models underscore the centrality of financial behaviours as the most significant factor directly influencing financial wellbeing. They also illustrate the various factors that affect financial wellbeing both directly and indirectly, primarily by influencing behaviours. These factors include financial knowledge and skills, personal dispositions, financial background and contextual elements. In reviewing these models, the chapter sheds light on the theoretical and empirical underpinnings that guide the current research efforts around this phenomenon.

While these models effectively map the research landscape, they are less useful for guiding practical applications. The pathways model introduced in the next chapter offers an innovative framework that can be used for guiding applied work.

7 A Novel Model of Financial Wellbeing

This chapter introduces a novel model of financial wellbeing, grounded in the principles of Positive Economic Psychology: A Pathways Model of Financial Wellbeing. This applied framework serves as a practical blueprint for action. The previous chapter highlighted the considerable advancements in our understanding of the theoretical underpinnings of financial wellbeing, as well as its drivers and consequences, as captured by leading models. However, it also acknowledged a significant gap in the application of these insights, noting the absence of applied models that offer practical, evidence-based blueprints for improving financial wellbeing. In response to this gap, this chapter proposed an innovative model that synthesises psychological and economic principles, theoretical insights and empirical work to provide actionable pathways to financial wellbeing.

Rooted in the principles of Positive Economic Psychology, the model adopts a humanistic perspective, assuming that individuals are inherently capable of making wise and ethical economic decisions and engaging in effective behaviours. However, it also recognises the extensive body of research in Economic Psychology that highlights human economic shortcomings (Thaler, 2015; Kahneman et al., 2021). Rather than disregarding these findings, the model proposes a method to overcome these limitations.

The model also adheres to the principles of Positive Economic Psychology by highlighting adaptive and effective economic behaviours, offering a blueprint for achieving financial wellbeing, using constructive language, maintaining a non-prescriptive approach and targeting non-clinical individuals as its primary audience.

Crucially, the model incorporates components firmly rooted in contemporary research on the determinants of financial wellbeing. Each component delineates elements that have been empirically shown to enhance financial wellbeing.

The chapter commences by unpacking the key aims of the model and by considering who can use the model and for what purposes. Next, the two key theories that underpin the model are described. The following section describes the hierarchical model, examining each of its components and the connection between them. It then provides research evidence to support the

DOI: 10.4324/9781003415176-7

model. The chapter concludes by highlighting the limitations of the model and this body of research.

AIM

The aim of this model of financial wellbeing is twofold:

- To portray financial wellbeing by unpacking its various components, thereby providing a comprehensive understanding of what constitutes financial wellbeing.
- To serve as a practical roadmap for attaining, improving or maintaining financial wellbeing.

This dual-purpose approach enables individuals to gain insight into the key elements that contribute to financial wellbeing while also offering actionable strategies and pathways to enhance their financial health.

> Within this framework, **financial wellbeing** is conceptualised as a continuum reflecting an individual's subjective evaluation of the extent to which they have achieved a state of quality in the financial domain (Lomas et al., 2024) and incorporates both hedonic and eudaimonic dimensions. It can therefore be understood as a state in which people feel good about their financial situation while also functioning well economically (Salignac et al., 2020).

An important point to make is that the model aims to help people attain optimal financial wellbeing, a term which should not be misconstrued as an ideal or perfect state of financial wellbeing. Optimal financial wellbeing refers to a realistic and achievable state where individuals effectively manage their finances to meet their needs, achieve their financial goals and maintain a sense of security and stability. It is therefore seen as a dynamic and adaptable state that allows for adjustments in response to changing circumstances and life events.

Applying the Model

The primary application of this model is to support people in achieving an optimal state of financial wellbeing. This involves not only meeting basic financial needs but also attaining a level of financial security and prosperity that allows individuals to lead fulfilling and stress-free lives.

The framework can be utilised by practitioners, including counsellors, therapists, coaches, mentors and financial planners, to guide their client-facing work. Additionally, individuals and families can apply the model to understand the essence of financial wellbeing and follow its pathways to enhance their financial state. In the context of research, the model can direct future investigations and steer the development of novel financial wellbeing interventions and policies.

UNDERPINNING THEORIES

The proposed conceptual model draws on two prominent theories: Hope Theory (Snyder, 1994) and the Transtheoretical Model of Behavioural Change (Prochaska & Prochaska, 2019) (see details below). These were chosen as underpinning theories due to their applied perspective: while Hope Theory offers a guide for action, the Transtheoretical Model underlines the hierarchical structure of the model.

Hope Theory

Hope is a motivational concept linked to the pursuit of goals. According to Snyder's (1994) Hope Theory, hope is experienced when there is a strong desire to achieve a goal and a clear path to accomplish it.

Hope is defined as a positive motivational state in which an individual has established a goal, is motivated to pursue it and has formulated a plan to achieve it (Snyder et al., 2005). Hence, hope comprises two components:

- **Agency/Will:** A person's motivation to pursue a desired goal.
- **Pathways/Ways:** The strategies the individual has devised to achieve the goal.

Hope is, therefore, future-oriented and goal-focused. Additionally, hope encompasses an element of confidence underlying both its dimensions: the confidence in one's own ability to achieve a particular goal and the effectiveness of the planned strategies (Snyder et al., 2005).

Hope becomes especially significant when the attainability of goals is uncertain, and the goals are perceived as highly important. Individuals who exhibit hope as a trait tend to set more challenging goals and are more likely to achieve them. This is attributed not only to their determination but also to their pathways thinking, which facilitates goal attainment.

Hope theory has been integrated into the proposed model to elicit pathways thinking: the will and the way. The first tier of the model represents the will to achieve financial wellbeing, while the next tiers chart the ways to achieve financial wellbeing.

The Transtheoretical Model of Behavioural Change

The Transtheoretical Model of Behavioural Change (Prochaska & Prochaska, 2019) provides a comprehensive framework for understanding and promoting behaviour change across various domains. The model addresses self-initiated changes, such as adopting new dietary habits, quitting smoking, altering exercise routines or modifying consumption patterns. It outlines the typical process that individuals undergo when initiating these changes. The model originated from research into health behaviours (particularly focusing on overcoming substance abuse, including alcohol, smoking and drug use).

According to Prochaska et al. (2015), behavioural changes often progress through the following stages:

- **Pre-contemplation:** In this initial phase, individuals are unaware of the need for change and have no intention to take action. They might have information about their condition, but choose to ignore it. For example, a person may know they are overspending but have no intention to budget or save.
- **Contemplation:** At this stage, individuals recognise the need for change and begin to consider taking action. They gather information, consult others and explore different pathways to change. However, they remain ambivalent and do not make a commitment. For instance, a person might learn about budgeting and saving methods but has not yet decided to implement them.
- **Preparation:** Individuals decide to initiate change, become aware of the costs and benefits and develop an action plan. They may start experimenting with changes, taking small steps to increase their determination. Examples include planning to create a budget, consulting a financial adviser, opening a savings account or setting up strategies to reduce spending.
- **Action:** In this stage, individuals begin to implement their plan and modify their behaviour. This can involve a single step or a series of actions. For instance, at this stage a person might start tracking expenses, adhere to a budget, make regular savings deposits and practise self-discipline in spending.
- **Maintenance:** This phase, often considered the longest, involves actively working to sustain the new behaviour and prevent relapses. A person might need to manage temptations to overspend or deal with unexpected financial challenges to maintain their budgeting and saving efforts.
- **Termination:** At this final stage, the new behaviour becomes habitual and normative, with minor risks of relapse. The person now identifies as financially responsible and has no desire to return to previous poor financial habits.

Substantial evidence suggests that behavioural change occurs in stages. However, this progression is not linear but cyclical. The process involves both advancement from one stage to the next and periodic relapses. The model indicates that even when change is ultimately successful, individuals will likely oscillate between the stages, experiencing one or more regressions before eventually reaching the termination stage. Understanding these phases and anticipating progress and regressions can help individuals begin their journey with more realistic expectations and persevere in achieving their goals.

The theory was integrated into the novel model by establishing a staged process (the six tiers) through which individuals can progress to achieve financial wellbeing. However, as the Transtheoretical Model suggests, the financial wellbeing model posits that advancement through these stages may not always be linear and can involve both progress and setbacks.

Together, Hope Theory and the Transtheoretical Model of Behavioural Change provide a complementary foundation for the proposed conceptual model. While Hope Theory foregrounds motivation and strategic goal pursuit that are essential for envisioning and striving towards financial wellbeing, the Transtheoretical Model introduces a structured, process-oriented understanding of behavioural change. Integrating these theories yields a model that is both aspirational and pragmatic: it acknowledges the importance of agency and pathways while recognising the dynamic, non-linear nature of personal change.

This dual-theoretical foundation ensures the model is psychologically grounded and applicable in real-world contexts. It supports the idea that achieving financial wellbeing is not a single act, but a gradual, iterative process influenced by motivation, planning and behavioural readiness. These insights inform both the model's structure and its practical utility, as detailed in the following sections.

THE MODEL

The model is hierarchical, comprising six tiers that build upon one another to collectively provide a blueprint for financial wellbeing (see Figure 7.1). It outlines each component and illustrates how these elements interact. Additionally, the model considers the economic contexts and personal

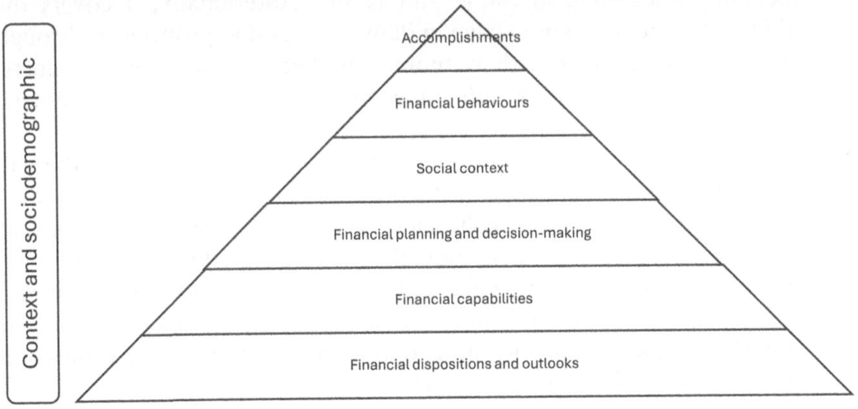

Figure 7.1 Pathways to financial wellbeing: a positive economic psychology model

factors that can influence each tier, suggesting that these should be taken into account at every stage in the pursuit of financial wellbeing.

- **Contextual and sociodemographic factors:** The contextual factors in the model, situated outside the hierarchy, primarily pertain to macro-level elements such as a country's economic strength, unemployment levels, monetary and social policies and the availability of financial services. Sociodemographic factors include elements such as age, gender, social status and life events. The model suggests that these factors can influence each tier and should be considered at every stage in the pursuit of financial wellbeing. However, these factors were purposely located outside the tiers as the model conveys a powerful message: while these factors should be considered and taken into account, they should not be viewed as immutable determinants.
- **Dispositions and outlooks:** Located at the bottom of the hierarchy, personality traits and financial attitudes serve as the essential foundation for all subsequent levels. It underscores the significance of one's core traits and perspectives towards the self and towards money, and suggests that these are likely to influence the willingness to acquire financial knowledge and skills, shape financial decisions and behaviours, and thereby indirectly affect a person's capacity to achieve financial wellbeing. The model posits that developing self-awareness and addressing limiting beliefs and habits is a crucial initial step in fostering healthy levels of financial wellbeing.
- **Financial capabilities:** The second tier builds upon the foundational dispositions and mindsets and focuses on the acquisition of financial literacy and skills and on engagement with the economic environment. This encompasses understanding economic concepts that can help individuals grasp their economic environment, such as financial policies, interest rates and inflation. It also involves developing practical financial skills, including budgeting, investing and saving. Additionally, it covers the ability to apply this knowledge in daily life, gaining proficiency through repeated engagement with economic markets, services and products. Mastery in this tier equips individuals to navigate the financial landscape effectively.

  It is notable that by positioning financial literacy and skills in the second tier (rather than the first), the model aligns with insights from academic research on financial literacy. The model reflects concerns that financial literacy alone does not always lead to effective behaviours, mainly due to the adverse effects of personal dispositions and attitudes (CFPB, 2015a). By establishing mindsets as the foundational tier, the model strategically aims to mitigate the impact of attitudes, values and beliefs on financial capabilities and behaviours.
- **Financial planning and decision making:** The third tier focuses on financial planning and decision-making. At this stage, individuals use their

financial capabilities and underlying mindsets to define meaningful short- and long-term goals and to make informed, intentional decisions and choices. This tier entails converting financial knowledge, skills and attitudes into strategic action by setting priorities, evaluating alternatives and managing the tension between immediate needs and future objectives. Effective planning and decision-making at this level may involve anticipating current and future financial demands, preparing for uncertainty, identifying opportunities and allocating resources and assets in a considered and efficient manner.

- **Social context:** The fourth tier introduces social context and responsibility as a guiding principle that influences financial decisions and behaviours. It highlights the social environment in which individuals operate financially, examining how this environment shapes financial attitudes, skills, decisions and behaviours, and how detrimental influences can be mitigated. It further acknowledges that financial decisions and behaviours carry implications not only for the individual but also for their family, community and society. Embracing social responsibility can enhance personal financial wellbeing by fostering an ethical environment, facilitating access to supportive networks and contributing to a more stable and equitable economic landscape.
- **Financial behaviours:** The fifth tier captures the practical expression of the earlier levels, representing the point at which financial outlooks, skills, planning and social awareness are translated into day-to-day action. At this stage, financial wellbeing is reflected in concrete behaviours, including diversifying income streams, saving regularly, spending prudently, making informed investment decisions, and managing debt effectively. This tier also includes the ongoing regulation of financial habits, the capacity to behave consistently with one's values and priorities and the maintenance of practices that promote both short-term stability and long-term resilience. In this sense, financial behaviours constitute the visible manifestation of the capabilities, dispositions and intentions developed in the preceding tiers.
- **Accomplishments:** At the pinnacle of the model, accomplishments represent the ultimate expression and outcomes of effective financial behaviours. This tier focuses on the realisation of financial goals and the achievement of a secure and satisfying financial state. Accomplishments include objective elements such as maintaining a stable income, having an emergency fund, pension savings, or securing appropriate insurance, as well as subjective factors like experiencing peace of mind and being able to enjoy life. These accomplishments manifest in an individual's quality of life, as well as contribute to communal and societal endeavours, hence reflecting the interconnected nature of personal and collective financial wellbeing.

Conclusion

The Positive Economic Psychology Pathways model to financial wellbeing presented in this section underscores the essential components for achieving financial wellbeing. By placing dispositions and outlooks as the foundational tier, the model highlights the psychological basis of financial behaviours as crucial for the success of subsequent financial literacy and behaviours. The model's comprehensive structure – from mindset through literacy, decision-making, social context and responsibility, behaviours, and ultimately, accomplishments, while taking into account contextual and sociodemographic factors – offers a holistic perspective of the individual within the economic environment.

Importantly, the model is designed as a practical tool for individuals and households to understand the core elements of financial wellbeing and follow its pathways to improve their financial health, and for practitioners to guide their client-facing work.

EVIDENCE SUPPORTING THE MODEL

This section reviews the evidence supporting the model. In doing so, it considers the extent to which the model is grounded in existing empirical literature and examines whether its key components and underlying assumptions are consistent with current knowledge in the field. The section also highlights existing gaps in the literature.

Sociodemographic and Contextual Factors

Sociodemographic variables such as gender, age, socioeconomic status, poverty and race have received limited attention in relation to financial wellbeing. These factors may affect financial wellbeing both directly and indirectly, with their effects often mediated by financial attitudes, literacy, behaviours and available resources (Mahendru et al., 2022). These variables provide a foundational understanding of how different segments of the population experience financial wellbeing and highlight disparities between various groups.

Macro-level factors have also attracted limited consideration in the research on financial wellbeing. These factors refer to the broader social, economic and structural conditions that shape the financial wellbeing of individuals, households, organisations and communities. They include economic policy, labour market conditions, welfare systems and social norms. These shape the economic landscape in which individuals and households operate, influencing their ability to achieve and maintain financial wellbeing.

By examining these factors, this section offers empirical support for the vertical axis of the pathways model. The model suggests that such factors may shape every tier. At the same time, it is important to emphasise that these factors are deliberately located outside the tiers of the model to communicate a central point: although they should be taken into account when setting financial goals, making decisions and plans and designing interventions, they should not be treated as determinants of financial wellbeing.

- **Age:** Several studies have examined the relationship between age and financial wellbeing, but their findings are mixed. Collins and Urban (2021) reported on a steady increase in financial wellbeing across the lifespan. By contrast, Comerton-Forde et al. (2018) found that financial wellbeing remains relatively stable from young adulthood to middle age, and rises between ages 50 and 70. Philippas and Avdoulas (2022) reported no significant association between age and financial wellbeing. Cross-national variations are also evident: older adults in Mexico report low financial wellbeing (Garcia-Mata et al., 2022), whereas retirees in Australia report the highest levels (Haisken-DeNew et al., 2018).

  What might account for these findings? One explanation is that financial knowledge and skills tend to increase with age, supporting more prudent financial behaviours and better outcomes at midlife (Lusardi et al., 2010; Taft et al., 2013). Evidence also points to income disparities across age groups, which can explain the differences between age groups in financial wellbeing: younger adults typically earn less than other groups, those in late middle age (45–54 years) report the highest incomes and the oldest group records the second-lowest incomes (DeNavas-Walt et al., 2013). In addition, younger people tend to hold more maladaptive financial beliefs, which may impair financial decision-making and constrain wealth accumulation, resulting in reduced financial wellbeing (Klontz et al., 2011; Castro-Gonzáles et al., 2020). These findings suggest that the association between age and financial wellbeing is mediated by financial knowledge, skills, behaviours and financial resources.
- **Gender:** Research on the association between gender and financial wellbeing remains limited, with existing studies indicating that men report higher levels of financial wellbeing compared to women (Fu, 2020).

  Women's lower financial wellbeing may stem from several factors. Research suggests women often have lower financial knowledge, which can reduce confidence, risk tolerance and engagement with financial matters (Chen & Volpe, 2002; Lusardi & Mitchell, 2014; Grohmann, 2016; Philippas & Avdoulas, 2022). Gender differences in money beliefs may also matter: men are more likely to link money with power, achievement and status, while women tend to focus more on saving or spending and report higher financial anxiety (Furnham et al., 2012; Pereira & Coelho, 2020; Tang, 1992). These patterns may decrease women's economic participation, leading to limited resources, low security and diminished financial wellbeing. Women's lower financial wellbeing is also linked to irregular work patterns, caregiving responsibilities and structural barriers such as the gender pay gap and glass ceiling (Goncalves et al., 2021).
- **Social class:** Socioeconomic status (SES) is typically measured using indicators such as education, employment and income (see Chapter 3), which tend to show similar findings to the associations reported between

education, employment and income (see below) and financial wellbeing. By contrast, research on subjective SES is scarce, with existing evidence indicating that higher parental social status is linked to better financial wellbeing in adulthood (Furnham & Cheng, 2017).

Social class shapes access to education, employment opportunities and social networks, all of which are vital for building financial resources (Spilerman, 2000; Brown, 2017). Those from higher social classes typically benefit from greater opportunities and stronger financial safety nets, while those from lower social classes are more likely to face poorer educational opportunities, lower-paid employment and weaker social networks, thereby restricting their economic prospects. Research also suggests that lower social class is associated with limited financial socialisation, which may include maladaptive money attitudes, low financial literacy and less effective financial behaviours (Soria et al., 2014; Gudmunson & Danes, 2011). Taken together, these factors may reproduce financial inequalities across generations and deepen class-based differences in financial wellbeing.

- **Race:** Although the role of ethnicity in financial wellbeing remains underexplored, some evidence suggests that race may matter, with White participants reporting higher financial wellbeing than other racial groups (Gutter & Copur, 2011).

  Several factors may explain these differences. A key cause is unequal financial resources: research consistently shows large income and wealth gaps, with White Americans earning more than Black and Hispanic Americans. Similar patterns appear in the UK despite narrower employment gaps in recent decades (Mirza & Warwick, 2024; Oliver & Shapiro, 2006). Financial literacy gaps also play a role, with White and Asian Americans scoring higher on financial literacy than Black and Hispanic Americans. These gaps are attributed to unequal access to education and financial information (Angrisani et al., 2021; Mitchell & Lusardi, 2011). Differences in financial socialisation, values and priorities may further widen the gaps in financial behaviour and resources (Gutter et al., 2014; Hawkins & Zuiker, 2019). Racial disparities in access to financial services also contribute to lower savings and weaker retirement planning, increasing financial insecurity and stress (Faber, 2019; Lee et al., 2022; Lusardi, 2012). Social Inequality Theory (Therborn, 2013) suggests that these patterns reflect broader structural barriers, including discrimination in employment, education, housing and access to financial and social services.
- **Poverty:** Research directly examining poverty and financial wellbeing is limited, likely because meeting the criteria for poverty inherently reflects low financial wellbeing (see Chapter 3). By contrast, there is extensive evidence linking poverty to stress. Recent reviews showed that deprivation creates chronic, toxic stress with serious consequences for physical and mental health (Breitenbach et al., 2021; Brisson et al., 2020).

The concept of Poverty-Related Stress (Wadsworth et al., 2011) indicates that stress is not only a result of poverty but also a force that can deepen financial hardship, creating a difficult cycle to escape. People living in poverty often face multiple, ongoing stressors, including violence, overcrowded housing, limited resources, environmental risks and discrimination (Haushofer & Salicath, 2023). Over time, these pressures can overwhelm the body's regulatory systems, damaging health, coping capacity and cognitive functioning (Mayo et al., 2022; Danese & McEwen, 2012). This wear and tear increases the risk of conditions such as cardiovascular disease, depression and suicidality (Schulz et al., 2012; Santiago et al., 2011; O'Connor & Kirtley, 2017).

Research shows that poverty-related stress has harmful effects across the life course. In children and adolescents, it can disrupt brain development, weaken cognitive resources and reduce school engagement and achievement (Monks et al., 2022; Holmes & Kiernan, 2013). In adults, it can undermine parenting (Cooper, 2021) and increase the risk of intimate partner violence while also restricting the means to leave abusive relationships (Gilroy et al., 2015). In older adults, poverty is associated with physical illness, frailty, cognitive decline, dementia, reduced functioning and depression (Hayajneh & Rababa, 2022; Chen & Cao, 2020; Trani et al., 2022). Without effective interventions, poverty-related stress can reinforce the intergenerational transmission of poverty, limiting upward mobility and resource accumulation (Hubler et al., 2015)

- **Macro-level factors:** The limited research that compared financial wellbeing across countries indicates that financial contexts matter (Riitsalu & van Raaij, 2022; Vasicek et al., 2017). However, the sources of these differences remain unclear. Some studies have examined GDP, but findings are mixed. Xin et al. (2020) found higher financial wellbeing in Malaysia compared to China despite similar GDP levels, attributing the difference to factors such as employment and education. Evidence on inequality is also limited, with Zagorski et al. (2014) finding no significant link between national inequality and financial wellbeing across EU countries.

  Culture also impinges on financial wellbeing. Riitsalu and van Raaij (2022) reported lower financial wellbeing in individualistic cultures compared to collectivist ones. Trust in government has also been linked to higher financial wellbeing (Barrafrem et al., 2021). Salignac et al. (2020) found that government policies, including those on university fees and retirement benefits, can affect financial wellbeing, with policy changes generating financial uncertainty and anxiety. Other studies have shown that access to financial services is positively associated with financial wellbeing (Nandru et al., 2021; Salignac et al., 2020).

In sum, this section shows that sociodemographic and contextual factors provide an important backdrop to financial wellbeing by shaping the opportunities, constraints and structural conditions within which financial lives unfold. Age, gender, social class, race, poverty and macro-level influences such as policy, culture and access to financial services all appear to affect financial wellbeing, both directly and indirectly, through their impact on financial knowledge, attitudes, behaviours, resources and life chances. At the same time, the evidence supports the model's position that these factors should be treated as contextual influences rather than fixed determinants. They help explain persistent disparities in financial wellbeing across groups, yet they do not fully dictate individual outcomes. This reinforces the value of the vertical axis of the model, which highlights how broader structural and social conditions interact with every tier of the pathway to financial wellbeing.

The practical implications are that individuals seeking to strengthen their financial wellbeing should recognise the broader circumstances that shape financial opportunities and constraints, while not assuming that these conditions make progress unattainable. In practice, this involves setting financial goals and strategies that are realistic and responsive to one's life stage, social position and economic environment, while also identifying structural disadvantages that may call for additional support, advocacy or tailored interventions. More broadly, the findings underline the importance of policy responses, including improved access to education, fair employment, financial services and social protection. Efforts to promote financial wellbeing should therefore combine personal agency with a clear awareness of the contextual conditions that can enable or constrain financial flourishing.

Dispositions and Outlooks

Research examining the relationship between personality and financial wellbeing is scarce. The limited literature has considered traits including the Big Five, self-regulation, self-efficacy, locus of control, optimism, time perspective and risk tolerance. While personality was once regarded as largely fixed, contemporary evidence indicates that it develops across the lifespan and can be modified through targeted interventions (McAdams & Olson, 2010; Roberts et al., 2017).

Money-related values, beliefs and attitudes, shaped by cultural, familial and personal experiences, influence individuals' financial aspirations, financial management practices and these in turn impact financial wellbeing.

This section reviews the research underpinning the first tier of the model, providing empirical support for its central claim that financial dispositions and mindsets form the foundation for the subsequent levels.

- **The Five Factor Model:** Research on the association between the Big 5 (conscientiousness, openness, neuroticism, extraversion and agreeableness) and financial wellbeing indicates that conscientiousness is associated with improved financial wellbeing, whereas neuroticism is linked to poor financial wellbeing (Coats & Bajtelsmit, 2024).

These traits seem to influence financial wellbeing primarily indirectly, through their effect on financial attitudes, literacy, behaviours and resources. Conscientiousness is associated with greater financial knowledge, disciplined behaviour, wealth accumulation and lower debt (Donnelly et al., 2012; Coats & Bajtelsmit, 2024). Conversely, neuroticism is linked to anxious money attitudes, low financial literacy, detrimental financial behaviours (compulsive purchasing and risky behaviours) (Coats & Bajtelsmit, 2024; Donnelly et al., 2012; Oehler & Wedlich, 2018) and lower income (Mueller & Plug, 2006). Interestingly, while not associated with financial wellbeing, the other Big-5 traits seem to be associated with financial behaviours and resources. Openness is associated with innovative financial behaviours (such as investing in emerging markets), and with higher levels of income and wealth (Mueller & Plug, 2006), but it is also linked to riskier financial decisions (Rai et al., 2021). Similarly, extraversion is associated with high risk tolerance in investment activities (Oehler & Wedlich, 2018), but is also associated with holding materialistic outlooks and with excessive buying (Otero-Lopez & Villardefrancos, 2013). Intriguingly, agreeableness is correlated with financial hardship, with researchers attributing this to the inclination to place low importance on money (Matz & Gladstone, 2020).

- **Self-efficacy:** Higher self-efficacy is associated with greater financial wellbeing (Fan & Henager, 2022).

  This relationship appears to operate largely through financial behaviour. A review by Furreboe and Nyhus (2022) found that high financial self-efficacy predicts prudent financial behaviours, including planning, saving, investing, responsible credit use and seeking financial advice. It is also associated with greater financial literacy, higher risk tolerance, greater use of financial products and wealth accumulation, whereas low self-efficacy is linked to financial vulnerability.
- **Locus of control:** Research on locus of control and financial wellbeing has shown mixed findings. Magli et al. (2021) found that an internal locus of control is associated with greater financial wellbeing, whereas Rafien et al. (2022) found no significant relationship.

  Locus of control may influence financial wellbeing both directly and indirectly, often through financial literacy and behaviour. Individuals with a stronger internal locus of control are more likely to acquire financial knowledge, make informed decisions, plan ahead, engage in sensible financial behaviours and show high risk tolerance (Chujan et al., 2022; Perry & Morris, 2005), and it has also been linked to higher income and wealth (Furnham & Cheng, 2017).
- **Self-control:** Self-discipline has been associated with higher financial wellbeing (Bai, 2023).

The primary ways in which self-regulation influences financial wellbeing are through its effects on financial literacy, decision-making and behaviours. Research suggests that individuals with strong self-discipline tend to have higher financial literacy, engage in more careful planning and decision-making and display more judicious financial behaviours, which contribute to their financial resources (Mpaata et al., 2023; Stromback et al., 2017). By contrast, impulsivity is associated with impulse buying, problematic credit behaviours, over-indebtedness and with gambling (Elliott et al., 2023; Fenton-O'Creevy et al., 2018; Nower & Blaszczynski, 2006).

- **Risk tolerance:** Research on the association between risk tolerance and financial wellbeing has produced inconsistent findings. While Kumar et al. (2023) found that greater risk tolerance is linked to improved financial wellbeing, Mathew et al. (2024) observed that high risk tolerance is associated with lower financial wellbeing.

  Risk tolerance appears to influence financial wellbeing mainly through its effects on financial behaviour and financial resources. Research suggests that higher risk tolerance is associated with the use of wealth-building strategies, such as investing and saving, which contribute to higher net worth (Song et al., 2023).
- **Optimism:** The few available studies that examined the association between optimism and financial wellbeing reported that optimism is associated with high financial wellbeing (Ianole-Calin et al., 2021).

  What might account for this association? Optimism has been linked to positive outcomes across several life domains, including employment, income and wealth (Gladstone & Pomerance, 2025; Mohanty, 2012; Segerstrom, 2007). It is also associated with healthy self-esteem, self-efficacy, planning, motivation and persistence (Segerstrom et al., 2017), which can support goal-directed behaviour and successful outcomes (Lim & Bone, 2022). In response to adversity, optimists tend to use more adaptive coping strategies, including problem-focused, preventive and proactive approaches, whereas pessimists are more likely to rely on maladaptive strategies such as distraction and denial (Forgeard & Seligman, 2012). These differences may also shape responses to financial adversity. However, findings on optimism and financial behaviour produced contrasting findings. Some studies found no association between optimism and financial behaviours (Hashmi et al., 2021) or with wealth-building strategies (Grevenbrock, 2020), while others suggested that optimism may be linked to higher debt, lower wealth, unemployment (Balasuriya et al., 2016) and to inadequate insurance coverage (Coats & Bajtelsmit, 2021). This suggests that the effects of optimism may depend on its degree, with over-optimism potentially leading to poorer financial outcomes (Kahneman, 2011).
- **Time orientation:** Researchers have argued that achieving financial wellbeing necessitates focusing on long-term financial security, making

a future time perspective an important factor (Hershfield et al., 2011). However, findings are mixed: a large study across 16 countries found that future time orientation is associated with greater financial wellbeing (Riitsalu & van Raaij, 2020), whereas Kempson et al. (2017) found no significant association.

Research indicates that time orientation influences financial literacy, financial decisions and behaviours, thereby affecting financial wellbeing indirectly. Future-oriented individuals are more likely to pursue financial education, make responsible decisions and engage in judicious financial behaviours, including wealth-building strategies such as saving, retirement planning and responsible borrowing (Antonides et al., 2011; Howlett et al., 2008; Joireman et al., 2005; Kooij et al., 2018). Time perspectives can also affect career trajectory and work, with future-oriented individuals being more likely to engage in long-term planning and undertake education and skill development opportunities (Guthrie et al., 2009). By contrast, present- or past-oriented individuals are more prone to impulsive spending, poor financial decisions and debt accumulation (Hershfield et al., 2011; Joireman et al., 2005).

- **Materialism:** The few studies that examined the relationship between materialism and financial wellbeing reported that materialism is associated with low financial wellbeing (Gutter & Copur, 2011). Minimalism, often viewed as the opposite of materialism, has been linked to improved financial wellbeing (Malik & Ishaq, 2023).

  Several explanations have been proposed for this relationship. Sirgy (1998) argued that materialistic individuals are more likely to engage in upward social comparison, which can reduce their financial satisfaction. Kasser (2018) suggested that the pursuit of materialistic goals may undermine the fulfilment of basic psychological needs. For example, striving for wealth can lead to working long hours or taking additional employment, thereby reducing time available for social interactions and compromising the satisfaction of social needs.

  Research also suggests that materialism affects financial wellbeing primarily indirectly, through its influence on financial attitudes and behaviours. Materialism has been associated with maladaptive money beliefs, such as viewing money as a symbol of power, status and prestige, as well as with anxious money attitudes (Pilch & Gornik-Durose, 2017). Materialism is also linked to ineffective financial behaviours such as low savings, poor money management, compulsive buying, overconsumption and higher debt, which contribute to financial strain (Gardarsdottir & Dittmar, 2012; Kasser, 2018).
- **Money beliefs:** Studies have reported that retentive financial attitudes – linking money to security and effort-based success – are associated with higher financial wellbeing (Sabri et al., 2020). Pragmatic attitudes such as saving orientation, spending control and avoiding debt were found to promote financial wellbeing (Sabri et al., 2020; Ponchio et al., 2019).

Money beliefs can have a direct impact on financial wellbeing. For example, anxious money beliefs involve negative emotions and concerns about security, leading to a lower subjective assessment of one's financial wellbeing. Additionally, these attitudes can influence financial wellbeing indirectly by shaping financial literacy, decisions, behaviours and resources. Several studies reported that beliefs that emphasise caution and prudence in financial decisions and actions, and the belief that money provides safety and security, are linked to improved financial literacy and responsible financial behaviours including money management, regular saving, adequate insurance coverage, sensible credit use, disciplined shopping habits and maintaining low levels of debt (de Almeida et al., 2021; Von Stumm et al., 2013a; Henchoz et al., 2019; Castro-González et al., 2020; Klontz & Britt, 2012). Beliefs that link money to power are associated with working hard to earn money. However, this belief is also linked to workaholism (Klontz & Britt, 2012).

Conversely, emotional discomfort in financial matters, seeing money as a means to evaluate success and viewing money as a source of evil have been linked to ineffective financial behaviours such as lack of planning, budgeting, monitoring and goal setting, low self-control, excessive credit use and risk taking (Klontz et al., 2011; Fenton-O'Creevy & Furnham, 2020a; Pereira & Coelho, 2020).

Cautious money beliefs are linked to higher income and wealth (Klontz & Britt, 2012), whereas the perception that self-worth is determined by net worth produced mixed results regarding its association with income (Klontz et al., 2011, 2015), but is linked with lower-wealth (Klontz et al., 2011). This perception has also been identified as a predictor of financial disorders such as gambling and workaholism (Klontz & Britt, 2012). Beliefs linking money to freedom, power and success have been linked to financial difficulties (Von Stumm et al., 2013b). Klontz et al. (2011) also found that believing that money is a source of evil is linked to lower income and wealth.

As for ethical financial perceptions, research suggests that individuals who view money as a source of evil are less likely to tolerate unethical behaviours (Tang & Chiu, 2003), whereas the love of money and beliefs linking money with status are associated with unethical intentions or behaviours (Chen et al., 2014; Klontz & Britt 2012).

- **Financial disorders:** By their very nature, financial disorders such as gambling, workaholism, compulsive buying and hoarding tend to induce financial stress, since they result in diminishing resources, excessive debt and economic instability. However, there is scarce empirical research exploring the link between these disorders and financial wellbeing or stress. The research indicates that compulsive buying is associated with poor financial wellbeing (Ozer et al., 2017), and gambling is linked to elevated levels of debt-related financial stress (Swanton & Gainsbury, 2020).

This section positions dispositions and outlooks as the foundational tier in the pathway to financial wellbeing. Although the evidence base remains limited in some areas, the overall pattern suggests that traits, beliefs and outlooks shape how individuals interpret financial matters, acquire financial knowledge, make decisions and behave in financial contexts. Factors such as conscientiousness, self-efficacy, self-control, optimism, future orientation and prudent money beliefs appear to support financial wellbeing, whereas neuroticism, impulsivity, materialism, maladaptive money beliefs and financial disorders tend to undermine it. The section, therefore, reinforces the model's central claim that financial wellbeing begins not with financial products or techniques alone, but with the psychological dispositions and outlooks that influence whether knowledge and opportunities are translated into beneficial actions.

For those pursuing their financial wellbeing, these findings suggest that progress may depend as much on psychological self-awareness as on financial knowledge. In practice, this means identifying personal tendencies, beliefs and emotional patterns that may support or hinder sound financial behaviour, such as impulsivity, avoidance, over-optimism, materialistic striving, or anxious money beliefs. Strengthening dispositions such as self-efficacy, self-control and future orientation, while cultivating more balanced and constructive beliefs about money, may create a stronger foundation for planning, learning and decision-making. Thus, efforts to improve financial wellbeing should include reflective and behavioural work on mindset and habits.

Financial Capabilities

Financial capabilities comprise a range of competencies, including education, financial knowledge, practical skills and financial inclusion (Xiao et al., 2022). Together, these enable individuals to make informed decisions, navigate financial systems and manage their finances effectively.

The review below focuses on the second tier of the model, which concerns the developmental pathway to financial wellbeing through the acquisition of financial capabilities. Equally important, however, is the ability to apply this knowledge in real-life contexts, developing proficiency through experience and repeated practice.

- **Education:** Research links higher levels of education with greater financial wellbeing (Comerton-Forde et al., 2022).

  Researchers have identified several pathways through which education may shape financial wellbeing. One explanation is that education improves access to employment opportunities and, consequently, affects income level and financial stability. Studies have reported that higher educational attainment is associated with better-paid jobs and increased earnings (Tamborini et al., 2015; Walker & Zhu, 2003). Education also strengthens financial literacy and numeracy (Philippas & Avdoulas,

2022). In addition, people with higher levels of education are more likely to engage in prudent financial behaviours, such as planning, saving and investing (Girshina, 2019; Philippas & Avdoulas, 2022).

Studies also point to differences by field of study. Graduates in economics, business, accounting and financial planning tend to have higher earnings and stronger job security (Dwyer et al., 2012). Their academic training seems to provide stronger financial literacy, which can support more effective financial management, including debt repayment, saving and investing (Britton et al., 2016; Dwyer et al., 2012). By contrast, graduates in the social sciences, humanities and arts often face lower earnings, slower career progression and less exposure to formal financial education, which may contribute to weaker financial behaviours, such as delayed saving and investing (de Vries, 2014; Dwyer et al., 2012).

Some research further suggested that highly educated individuals are more likely to associate money with power and success, whereas those with lower levels of education tend to report more money-related anxiety (Fenton-O'Creevy & Furnham, 2020b). However, other studies have found no clear link between education and financial beliefs (Tang, 1995; Von Stumm et al., 2013a).

- **Financial knowledge:** Studies have reported that high objective financial literacy (as measured through knowledge tests) is associated with increased financial wellbeing (Zhang & Chatterjee, 2023), but a stronger association was found between subjectively assessed financial knowledge and financial wellbeing (Xiao et al., 2024).

  Financial literacy is thought to influence financial wellbeing indirectly by encouraging more prudent attitudes and behaviours. Research evidence suggests that individuals with higher levels of objective or subjective financial literacy are more likely to set financial goals, plan ahead, track expenses, budget, pay bills on time, save, insure, maintain emergency funds, contribute to retirement savings, secure lower-cost loans, invest and diversify risk (Kempson et al., 2017; Lusardi & Mitchell, 2007; Murendo & Mutsonziwa, 2017; van Rooij et al., 2011; 2012). It is also associated with greater financial confidence (Lone & Bhat, 2024), stronger participation in financial markets (Grohmann et al., 2018), greater use of financial technology (Yoshino & Morgan, 2020), higher risk tolerance (Song et al., 2023) and better resilience in coping with economic strain (Klapper & Lusardi, 2020). These behaviours and capacities can, in turn, contribute to better financial outcomes, including greater wealth accumulation (Behrman et al., 2012). In contrast, low financial literacy can lead to poor debt decisions, such as high-cost borrowing and unsuitable loan or mortgage choices, which may result in over-indebtedness, mortgage delinquency and foreclosure (Gerardi, 2010; Lusardi et al., 2011; Lusardi & Tufano, 2015).

  However, these findings have been challenged. Riitsalu et al. (2023) argued that individuals often disregard financial information, and there is evidence to suggest that people may display competent financial behaviours despite limited knowledge, while those with strong financial understanding do not always act in ways that support their financial wellbeing. Similarly, Rothwell et al. (2018) contended that factual knowledge does not necessarily translate into sensible action or behavioural change, because the link between knowledge and behaviour is shaped by personal traits, attitudes and circumstances, which may lead individuals to act against their better judgement.

- **Financial skills:** Although research on financial skills and financial wellbeing is limited, existing evidence suggests that greater financial capability is associated with higher financial wellbeing (CFPB, 2015a). In particular, skills such as budgeting, saving, investing and knowing how to access financial advice are positively related to financial wellbeing (Collins & Urban, 2021). Digital financial skills have also been found to predict financial wellbeing (Kamble et al., 2024).

  The relationship between financial skills and financial wellbeing appears to be mediated by dispositions and financial behaviours. Research indicates that stronger financial capability is associated with greater self-efficacy (Reyers, 2019), though not necessarily with money beliefs (Von Stumm et al., 2013b). Higher financial skills are also linked to better financial decisions and behaviours, including planning, budgeting, saving and investing (Nosratabadi et al., 2019; Reyers, 2019). Digital financial skills, in particular, are associated with greater financial inclusion, suggesting that they improve access to financial markets and products (Kumar et al., 2023). Financial capability is also related to better financial outcomes, including higher income and wealth (Fenton-O'Creevy & Furnham, 2022; Von Stumm et al., 2013b).

  At the same time, similar to financial literacy, critics have noted that possessing financial skills does not guarantee that they will be used effectively. Hebert and Gyarmati (2014) argued that applying these skills requires motivation, willingness to invest time and resources, engagement with relevant markets, confidence in one's abilities and resilience in the face of obstacles. Relatedly, Gignac (2022) found that individuals with lower financial ability are more likely to overestimate their competence than those with higher ability. This overconfidence can contribute to harmful financial outcomes, including excessive risk-taking, overspending and indebtedness.
- **Financial inclusion:** Access to and use of financial services and products, as well as active participation in economic markets, are seen as essential for managing and accumulating resources (Demirguc-Kunt et al., 2018). Although there is scarce research on its link with financial wellbeing, existing studies suggest that greater financial inclusion is associated with higher financial wellbeing, partly because it enables people to manage their financial affairs more effectively (Rashid et al., 2022).

> Financial inclusion appears to affect financial wellbeing mainly through its influence on financial decisions and behaviours. Research shows that use of financial products and services is associated with more prudent financial behaviours, likely because it builds mastery over time (Kempson et al., 2017). Studies also indicated that people with access to financial services tend to show better financial decision-making, greater confidence in managing their finances, stronger financial resilience and increased financial stability and security (Kempson et al., 2017). Importantly, financial access is linked to a lower likelihood of material hardship and poverty (Mosley & Lenton, 2012), whereas financial exclusion is associated with lower savings, over-indebtedness and greater vulnerability to financial shocks (Berlinger et al., 2021).

This section highlights financial capabilities as a crucial developmental tier in the pathway to financial wellbeing. Education, financial knowledge, practical skills and financial inclusion each appear to support financial wellbeing by strengthening people's ability to understand financial matters, engage with financial systems and make informed choices. At the same time, the evidence also makes clear that capability alone is not sufficient. Knowledge and skills do not automatically translate into beneficial financial behaviours. This justifies the model's placement of financial capabilities after dispositions and outlooks, while also underscoring their central role in enabling individuals to act effectively in pursuit of financial wellbeing.

For individuals seeking to improve their financial wellbeing, the findings highlight the importance of building financial capabilities in a broad and applied sense. This involves not only acquiring financial knowledge but also developing practical skills such as budgeting, saving, investing, comparing financial products and using digital financial tools with confidence. Equally important is active engagement with the financial systems through appropriate banking, credit, insurance and savings products. However, individuals should also recognise that meaningful progress requires self-awareness, motivation and the discipline to apply financial knowledge consistently in everyday life.

Financial Planning and Decision-Making

Financial planning and decision-making are seen as cognitive behaviours that empower individuals to take charge of their finances, while harmonising financial objectives and decisions with needs and life goals.

The review offered next addresses the third tier of the model, which concerns financial planning and decision making, drawing on earlier tiers – adaptive dispositions and outlooks and adept financial capabilities – to ensure that financial planning and decision making generate the desired results.

- **Financial planning:** Although financial planning is frequently presented as a crucial means for achieving financial wellbeing, there is scarce literature that examines the association between them. The available evidence indicates that financial planning is associated with greater financial wellbeing (Haisken-DeNew et al., 2018; Comerton-Forde et al., 2022). Across these studies, financial planning entailed the following behaviours: setting financial goals, forecasting future needs and expenses, devising strategies to achieve financial goals, budgeting and monitoring.

  There are several pathways through which financial planning may contribute to financial wellbeing. Studies have indicated that financial planning fosters prudent financial behaviours (Castro-González et al., 2020). Notably, studies reported that financial planning is associated with higher levels of wealth (Ameriks et al., 2003; Lusardi and Mitchell, 2007). Similarly, Lee and Kim (2016) reported that households with a stronger propensity to plan were better prepared for retirement in terms of their financial resources, while Lusardi (1999) found that individuals who did not engage in retirement planning had lower levels of financial wealth than those who did.

  However, there is also evidence that the relationship may be bidirectional. On the one hand, planning may support the accumulation of financial resources; on the other, individuals with greater economic resources may be more likely to engage in planning (Xiao & O'Neill, 2018). Financial planning may also affect financial wellbeing through its influence on perceived control. MacLeod et al. (2008) found that financial planning is associated with a stronger sense of control, which is recognised as a component of financial wellbeing.
- **Financial decisions:** Similar to financial planning, modest research has examined the relationship between financial decision-making and financial wellbeing, despite the central importance of such decisions in everyday financial life. The existing evidence suggests that deliberate and careful financial decision-making is associated with better financial wellbeing (Parvathy & Kumar, 2022). Accordingly, Comerton-Forde et al. (2022) found that delays in making financial decisions are associated with poorer financial wellbeing.

  Although it seems reasonable to assume that financial decision-making affects financial wellbeing indirectly through its influence on market participation and financial behaviours, there is no empirical research that has explored this point. Studies that focused on decision styles identified a positive association between a maximising decision-making style – the tendency to search for the best option – and financial wellbeing (Silber et al., 2024). Lamas and Murphy (2021), meanwhile, examined the use of financial rules of thumb and their relationship with financial wellbeing. Their findings indicated that some heuristics, such as paying off debt in full whenever possible and avoiding expenditure beyond one's means, were associated with better financial wellbeing. By contrast, other rules, including finding ways to earn extra money, rebalancing one's portfolio annually and paying oneself first, were associated with poorer financial wellbeing.

Taken together, this section highlights financial planning and decision-making as central mechanisms through which individuals translate financial attitudes, knowledge and skills into action. Although the empirical literature remains limited, the available evidence indicates that planning and careful decision-making are associated with stronger financial wellbeing, partly through their links with prudent financial behaviour, wealth accumulation, retirement preparedness and a greater sense of control. At the same time, the findings indicate that these relationships may be bidirectional, with existing financial resources also shaping the motivation to plan. Overall, this tier of the model underscores that financial wellbeing is advanced by the ability to convert skills and knowledge into intentional, goal-aligned financial strategies and decisions.

For those aiming to bolster their financial wellbeing, these findings point to the importance of approaching finances proactively rather than reactively. This involves setting clear financial goals, anticipating future needs and expenses, budgeting consistently and reviewing progress over time. More broadly, individuals may benefit from viewing financial planning as an ongoing process that can strengthen both objective financial outcomes and a subjective sense of control, thereby supporting greater financial wellbeing over time.

Social Context

This section dives into the fourth tier of the model: social context. At this pivotal stage in the journey towards financial wellbeing, individuals are called to step beyond their personal interests and consider how their social context influences their financial actions, decisions and outcomes, as well as the ripple effects of their own financial actions on others.

- **Relationship status:** Studies have shown that married individuals report higher financial wellbeing than those who are single, separated, divorced or widowed (Collins & Urban, 2021). Recent separation, illness and bereavement have been linked to declines in financial wellbeing (Comerton-Forde et al., 2022). Financial wellbeing also appears to decrease as the number of dependents increases, particularly where individuals have substantial caring responsibilities that interfere with work (Comerton-Forde et al., 2022; Haisken-DeNew et al., 2018).

  Several factors may help explain these findings. One possible explanation is resource pooling (Vogler & Pahl, 1994), whereby married individuals combine both financial and non-financial resources, including income, time and skills, in ways that enhance economic efficiency and stability. Pooling can increase purchasing power, lower costs, strengthen financial resilience, support the pursuit of shared financial goals and improve access to credit and other financial services. At the same time, it can also generate tensions, particularly where there are disagreements over how resources are allocated or where contributions are perceived to be unequal (Pahl, 1995).

A further explanation is that marriage may strengthen financial motivation. A heightened sense of responsibility towards a partner or family can encourage individuals to develop their financial capabilities and adopt more prudent financial behaviours (McDonald, 2020). However, as the number of dependents increases, financial strain also rises. Research indicates that although parents often face reduced disposable income, those who engage in financial planning and budgeting seem to sustain higher levels of financial wellbeing (Grinstein-Weiss et al., 2008).

A further explanation is the Marriage Premium phenomenon (Gedara, 2021), which indicates that married individuals, particularly men, tend to earn higher wages than their single counterparts (Gedara, 2021). This suggests that income may mediate the relationship between marital status and financial wellbeing. Finally, financial risk tolerance also appears to vary by relationship status. Single individuals, who often have fewer financial responsibilities, tend to be more willing to take financial risks (Grable & Joo, 2004), whereas married individuals are generally more inclined to prioritise the protection of wealth (Chaulk et al., 2003).

- **Financial socialisation:** Research has shown that effective financial socialisation is positively associated with financial wellbeing (Fan & Park, 2021). In particular, the quality of parent–child communication about financial matters has been identified as a central component of effective financial socialisation and a strong predictor of financial wellbeing later in life (Shim et al., 2015).

  At the same time, scholars suggested that financial socialisation influences financial wellbeing largely indirectly, through its effects on money attitudes, financial literacy, financial skills and financial behaviours. The family is the primary agent of financial socialisation, with parents playing a pivotal role in shaping children's financial beliefs, knowledge and behaviours. Research suggests that discussing money openly and involving children in financial activities can encourage the adoption of adaptive money beliefs, develop children's money management skills, strengthen their financial self-efficacy and lead to more responsible financial behaviours in adulthood (Jorgensen & Savla, 2010).

  Beyond the family, peers, schools and the media also serve as important agents of financial socialisation. Peer influence, depending on the financial habits and norms of the group, can either reinforce or undermine positive financial beliefs, knowledge and behaviours (Dangol & Maharjan, 2018; Reniers et al., 2017).

Positive financial socialisation helps children develop financial capabilities, constructive beliefs about money and responsible financial practices such as budgeting and saving, while also reducing the risk of excessive debt (Pak et al., 2023). By contrast, poor financial socialisation has been associated with financial mismanagement, risky financial behaviours, overspending, low levels of saving, debt, poor investment choices and greater financial insecurity (Gudmunson & Danes, 2011).

- **Social support:** Empirical research on the association between social support and financial wellbeing is scarce. The studies that have explored these links have done so primarily from the perspective of the recipients of support. Researchers have reported that higher levels of received social support are associated with greater financial wellbeing (Lambert et al., 2023), particularly in later life (Adam et al., 2017).

  These associations may be partly attributed to the influence of social support on behaviour, as the availability of social support is linked to responsible financial behaviours, such as budgeting and saving (Yulfa & Herawati, 2017).
- **Financial conflict:** The relationship between financial conflict and financial wellbeing has received meagre attention. Existing research has focused largely on the link between financial stress and financial conflict, typically examining how financial stress leads to discord rather than the reverse direction. In this work, financial stress is often portrayed as a trigger for money-related arguments between partners (Gajos et al., 2022). Communication appears to play an important moderating role in the association between financial stress and conflict, with constructive communication linked to greater financial harmony (Shebib & Cupach, 2018).
- **Social comparison:** Research has examined the relationship between social comparison and financial wellbeing, and the findings indicated that a tendency to engage in upward social comparison is associated with lower levels of financial wellbeing (Brown & Gray, 2016).

  The literature suggests that upward social comparison can undermine financial wellbeing directly by raising standards and expectations, thereby shaping self-evaluations of one's own financial state. It may also affect financial wellbeing indirectly through its influence on financial attitudes, decision-making, behaviour and financial resources. With regard to financial attitudes, several studies have found that a tendency to engage in upward social comparison is associated with higher levels of materialism (Zhang et al., 2016). Research also showed that social comparison can shape consumer behaviour across a range of consumption patterns, leading to increased spending (Drechsel-Grau & Greimel, 2024), stronger preferences for luxury goods and services (Lee & Watkins, 2016; Pillai & Nair, 2021), impulse buying (van Tran et al., 2023), compensatory consumption (Chowdhury & Swaminathan, 2024) and green or sustainable purchasing (Antonides, 2017). Social comparison can also foster competitive behaviour, as individuals seek social recognition, resources and status. Although upward comparison may motivate ambition and performance (Garcia et al., 2013), it can also intensify rivalry, particularly when success is perceived as a zero-sum game (Brown et al., 2007). This dynamic is especially evident in workplaces and in consumer markets, where people compare salaries, achievements and possessions (Suls et al., 2002). Social media may further amplify these pressures by presenting curated images of material success (Chou & Edge, 2012). These behaviours, in turn, can influence financial resources, with research linking upward social comparison to higher levels of debt (Kapeller & Schütz, 2015), lower savings (Zhang et al., 2016) and greater risk-taking in stock trading (Andraszewicz et al., 2023).

- **Engagement with social media:** A small number of studies have explored the relationship between social media usage and financial wellbeing, and reported that excessive social media engagement is negatively associated with financial wellbeing (She et al., 2023). Higher levels of fear of missing out are likewise linked to poorer financial wellbeing (Bartosiak et al., 2025). At the same time, some studies point to potential benefits, with research showing that receiving financial advice through social media can positively predict financial wellbeing (Gupta et al., 2025).

In sum, the evidence reviewed in this tier shows that financial wellbeing is deeply embedded in social relationships, roles and environments. Relationship status, financial socialisation, social support, financial conflict, social comparison and social media engagement all appear to influence financial wellbeing, either directly by affecting a person's self-perception of their situation, or indirectly by strengthening individuals' financial resources, skills and behaviours, or by exposing them to pressures, strains and risks that undermine financial security and satisfaction. This highlights the importance of viewing financial wellbeing as a socially situated phenomenon: one that is co-constructed through family dynamics, interpersonal communication, social norms and broader cultural influences. The social context tier, therefore, extends the earlier tiers of the model by showing that dispositions, skills and financial planning and decisions unfold within relational and societal settings that can either support or constrain financial wellbeing.

From a practical perspective, these findings suggest that individuals pursuing financial wellbeing should pay close attention to the social contexts in which their financial decisions and habits are formed and enacted. This means cultivating open and constructive communication about money within close relationships, recognising how family responsibilities and relationship dynamics may shape financial pressures and opportunities, and seeking supportive social networks that encourage sound financial behaviours. It also involves becoming more aware of the influence of financial socialisation, social comparison and social media on one's attitudes, expectations and spending decisions. Developing critical reflection around these influences, while strengthening financial habits, may help individuals resist unhelpful social pressures and make financial choices that are more closely aligned with their own values, goals and long-term wellbeing.

Financial Behaviours

Financial behaviours are widely regarded as critical predictors of financial wellbeing, encompassing several interrelated dimensions: earning behaviours, financial management behaviours, consumption and wealth-building. This section turns to the fifth tier of the model presented above, inviting individuals to reflect on their own actions and to recognise the ways in which these behaviours shape financial wellbeing.

- **Responsible financial behaviours:** Adaptive monetary behaviour is intentional, goal-directed action aimed at strengthening financial resources, enhancing security and stability and ultimately supporting financial wellbeing. Van Raaij (2016) suggested that such behaviours include spending less than one earns, retaining enough income to cover everyday expenses after obligatory payments, resisting impulsive purchases, making appropriate use of financial products and services, seeking professional advice when necessary, saving, managing credit and debt, mitigating risk through insurance and other strategies, investing and preparing for future uncertainties. These behaviours often require individuals to negotiate trade-offs, such as work and leisure, homeownership and renting, and saving and spending, while also balancing immediate and longer-term needs. Despite their clear practical importance, research examining the relationship between prudent financial behaviours and financial wellbeing remains limited. Existing evidence nevertheless indicates that such behaviours are among the strongest predictors of financial wellbeing (Xiao & Kim, 2022).

  Do these behaviours lead to improved financial outcomes, such as higher income and greater wealth? Research suggests that the association is bi-directional: prudent financial behaviours contribute to stronger financial resources, which in turn motivate further responsible financial behaviour (Goyal et al., 2021; Szendrey & Fiala, 2018). By contrast, careless or irresponsible financial behaviours can erode financial resources and increase financial instability and vulnerability (Xiao & O'Neill, 2018). Such behaviours are characterised by poor financial decision-making, inadequate planning, disorganised money management, impulsive or status-driven consumption, limited saving or investment and the accumulation of excessive debt (Fernandes et al., 2014). These patterns are often associated with low levels of financial literacy, cognitive and behavioural biases and social pressures that shape financial choices (Gathergood & Weber, 2017).

- **Earning behaviours and employment:** Although earning is a central financial behaviour, limited research has examined its relationship with financial wellbeing. The available evidence indicates that employment status is associated with financial wellbeing, with unemployed individuals reporting lower financial wellbeing than those who are employed (Comerton-Forde et al., 2022). In a study comparing workers across employment sectors, Mahdzan et al. (2023) found that public sector employees and self-employed individuals have the highest levels of financial wellbeing, private sector employees show slightly lower levels and unemployed individuals report the lowest levels of financial wellbeing. Similarly, Comerton-Forde et al. (2018) observed that retirees report the highest levels of financial wellbeing, followed by employees, students and unemployed individuals.

  Unemployment appears to be a particularly consequential life event for financial wellbeing. Loss of income often leads to deterioration in financial stability and increased reliance on savings or credit (Gallie & Paugam, 2000). The extent of this hardship is shaped by the duration of unemployment and the availability of social protections and informal support, such as unemployment benefits and family support (Kalleberg, 2011). Research on employment patterns and their relationship with financial wellbeing is also scarce. Evidence from studies of gig workers points to the difficulties associated with income volatility, with gig workers reporting lower financial wellbeing than both salaried employees and the self-employed (Peetz & Robson, 2021). By contrast, business ownership, despite its inherent risks and uncertainty, has been linked to higher financial wellbeing (Comerton-Forde et al., 2022). This pattern is not consistent across all groups, however. Guo and Huang (2023) found that low-income entrepreneurs experience lower financial wellbeing than higher-income entrepreneurs and this is linked to their lower financial knowledge, weaker financial skills and limited access to mainstream financial products, which leads them to depend on high-fee alternatives.
- **Financial management behaviours:** Few studies have examined the relationship between financial management behaviours and financial wellbeing. Overall, effective financial management practices seem to be associated with improved financial wellbeing (Philippas & Avdoulas, 2022), with financial organisation (Comerton-Forde et al., 2022), and budgeting and record-keeping (Bai, 2023), linked to higher levels of financial wellbeing. The evidence, however, is inconsistent. Some studies suggested that very tight budgeting and frequent financial monitoring are associated with lower financial wellbeing (Gutter & Copur, 2011), indicating that these behaviours may be beneficial only when exercised in moderation. With regard to bill payment, paying bills on time is linked to greater financial wellbeing, whereas missed or late payments are associated with poorer financial wellbeing (Comerton-Forde et al., 2022). In

relation to insurance, adequate insurance coverage has been found to be positively associated with financial wellbeing (Dong et al., 2019).

- **Consumption:** The evidence base on the relationship between consumption practices and financial wellbeing is small. Existing studies suggested that planned and disciplined spending behaviours, such as spending less than one's income, prioritising essential expenses and keeping records, are associated with higher financial wellbeing (Comerton-Forde et al., 2022; Kempson et al., 2017). By contrast, overspending, high levels of discretionary expenditure and living beyond one's means have been linked to poorer financial wellbeing (Comerton-Forde et al., 2022; Kempson et al., 2017). More generally, higher levels of expenditure have also been found to predict lower financial wellbeing (Kempson et al., 2017). The literature on conspicuous consumption indicates that it may function as a coping strategy among households experiencing income inequality, creating a false sense of financial wellbeing (Jaikumar et al., 2025). Relatedly, status-oriented consumption can encourage borrowing and contribute to indebtedness (Jaikumar & Sharma, 2021).
- **Wealth building:** Behaviours that are geared to build wealth include disciplined saving, prudent investing and careful debt management, which help to accumulate and protect financial resources over time. These practices can enhance resilience in the face of uncertainty, support opportunities for upward mobility and contribute to stronger financial wellbeing. However, there is scarce research examining the relationship between wealth-building behaviours and financial wellbeing.

  The available research indicates that saving behaviour is associated with higher financial wellbeing (Comerton-Forde et al., 2022). Among retirees, financial wellbeing is linked to the adequacy of retirement savings and the ability to manage expenses (Hershey et al., 2007). Individuals who engage in early and sustained retirement saving are more likely to achieve financial security and maintain their standard of living in later life. Conversely, inadequate retirement planning can lead to financial strain and lower financial wellbeing in retirement (Kim & Moen, 2002).

  Research on investment behaviours suggests that participation in stock market investing is positively associated with financial wellbeing (Comerton-Forde et al., 2022). Similarly, engagement in property investment is linked to higher levels of financial wellbeing (Comerton-Forde et al., 2022).

  Comerton-Forde et al. (2022) found that having a credit card is positively associated with financial wellbeing. However, Nagypal and Tobacman (2019) reported that greater credit card utilisation, a higher number of revolving accounts and recent debt collections are negatively associated with financial wellbeing. The literature also suggests that prudent borrowing, low levels of credit use and careful debt management, including paying debts and credit card balances on time, contribute to higher financial wellbeing (Collins & Urban, 2021). In contrast, risky borrowing practices, borrowing to cover essentials, or relying on credit for everyday expenses are associated with poorer financial wellbeing (Kempson et al., 2017). Comerton-Forde et al. (2022) further found that difficulty in meeting mortgage repayments is linked to lower financial wellbeing.

The available literature, though scarce, suggests that financial behaviours matter profoundly for financial wellbeing. Responsible, forward-looking behaviours, including stable earnings, effective financial management, disciplined consumption and sustained wealth-building, are associated with stronger financial wellbeing, whereas disorganisation, impulsivity and risky borrowing tend to undermine it. At the same time, the association between financial behaviours and financial wellbeing is often bi-directional: adaptive behaviours can strengthen financial resources and security, while stronger financial resources motivate adaptive behaviours.

A key practical implication is that improving financial wellbeing is rarely about making one major financial decision, but rather about developing consistent everyday habits that support greater stability, control and future security. From this perspective, individuals can strengthen their financial wellbeing by focusing on behaviours such as keeping spending within income, paying bills on time, monitoring credit use carefully, building regular savings habits and planning ahead for both expected and unexpected expenses. It is also important to recognise that financial wellbeing is shaped not only by how or how much money a person earns, but by how the available resources are managed. Improving financial wellbeing, therefore, involves reflecting on one's current financial behaviours, identifying unhelpful patterns such as impulsive spending or overuse of credit, and gradually replacing them with more deliberate, sustainable practices that align immediate needs with longer-term financial goals.

Achievements

Accomplishment is not an optional extra in a good life but a psychological necessity. Without the experience of pursuing valued goals and seeing progress, self-esteem weakens and motivation falters. Working towards success through setting goals, investing effort and monitoring progress fosters a sense of agency and mastery. By contrast, a life with few achievements can be demoralising, since it offers little evidence that one's actions make a difference (Deci & Ryan, 2000). Seligman (2012) argued that any credible theory of wellbeing should include accomplishment as a core component: the ability to turn intention and effort into meaningful outcomes. Financial wellbeing is no exception.

In the domain of financial wellbeing, accomplishments serve both as evidence of competence and as a foundation for further growth (Deci & Ryan, 2000). Their benefits are cumulative: each milestone builds experience, strengthens perceived capability, increases confidence, expands future options and sustains motivation for further effort. However, accomplishments are most beneficial when they are ethically grounded and psychologically integrated, that is, intrinsically motivated, acknowledged without arrogance, shared where appropriate and directed towards goals that matter beyond the self.

This section focuses on the apex of the financial wellbeing model: accomplishments. Accomplishments encompass objective markers – such as income and wealth, and subjective experiences – such as peace of mind. However, current evidence is only available on income and wealth.

- **Income:** Research on the relationship between income and financial wellbeing has yielded mixed findings. Collins and Urban (2021) found that higher income is associated with greater financial wellbeing. However, Zyphur et al. (2015) reported that income is positively associated with financial wellbeing only in men, Vlaev and Elliott (2014) found that the correlation between income and financial satisfaction is weak, and Haisken-DeNew et al. (2018) observed that although financial wellbeing generally rises with income, there is considerable variation among individuals at similar income levels. A decline in income is consistently linked to lower financial wellbeing (Comerton-Forde et al., 2022). In addition, Taylor et al. (2024) showed that fluctuations in employment and income during the years before retirement can have lasting and gendered effects on later-life financial wellbeing, with women tending to fare worse than men due to cumulative disadvantages in their employment trajectories. Evidence on government support suggests that reliance on welfare benefits is associated with lower financial wellbeing (Comerton-Forde et al., 2022).
- **Wealth:** The small number of studies examining wealth and financial wellbeing indicate that household net wealth and assets are important determinants of financial wellbeing (Brown & Gray, 2016). Relative wealth also appears to matter: Brown and Gray (2016) found that households report higher financial wellbeing when they perceive their financial position to be better than that of their reference group, and lower wellbeing when they perceive it to be worse. Savings, as a key indicator of wealth, have received limited attention, but existing evidence suggests that having an emergency fund or retirement savings is associated with higher financial wellbeing (Comerton-Forde et al., 2022). Among retirees, larger retirement savings balances are likewise linked to better financial wellbeing (Haisken-DeNew et al., 2018).

  In relation to investment, Comerton-Forde et al. (2022) found that owning a stock portfolio is positively associated with financial wellbeing.

  Higher credit scores and greater credit card limits are positively correlated with financial wellbeing (Nagypal & Tobacman, 2019). By contrast, debt predicts poor financial wellbeing (Brown & Gray, 2016), a finding supported by evidence that student loan debt is negatively associated with financial wellbeing (Nagypal & Tobacman, 2019).

The role of possessions has scarcely been explored, although home ownership has been found to be positively associated with financial wellbeing (Haisken-DeNew et al., 2018), whereas renting has been linked to lower financial wellbeing (Kempson et al., 2017).

In conclusion, the evidence reviewed in this section indicates that accomplishments in the financial domain, particularly income and wealth, are important components of financial wellbeing, but their effects are neither simple nor uniform, as the findings show that objective financial achievements do not translate automatically into financial wellbeing, since their effects vary across individuals and social groups and are shaped by life-course patterns, comparative standards and structural inequalities.

The implications for individuals pursuing financial wellbeing are that financial accomplishment is best approached as a gradual process. Individuals may benefit from focusing on attainable financial milestones, such as stabilising income where possible, building emergency savings, reducing problematic debt, improving credit management and preparing early for retirement. It is also important to evaluate financial progress against one's own needs and long-term goals rather than through comparison with others, since relative perceptions of income, wealth and possessions can distort judgements of wellbeing.

These findings invite reflection on one's financial goals, decisions and trajectory over time, assessing achievements and progress through criteria that reflect one's own background, needs, capacities, circumstances, values and financial and psychological outcomes.

Conclusion

Taken together, the evidence across the model provides qualified but meaningful support for its central proposition that financial wellbeing emerges not from any single factor, but through a layered pathway in which contextual conditions, psychological dispositions, financial capabilities, planning and decision-making, social influences, behaviours and accomplishments interact over time. The literature suggests that financial wellbeing is shaped by both objective circumstances and subjective interpretations, and by the dynamic interplay between personal agency and structural constraint. At the same time, the review reveals important gaps in the evidence base (see below), pointing to the need for further research. The model may therefore be viewed as a theoretically grounded and empirically informed framework that organises a fragmented literature, highlights key pathways and offers a basis for more integrative future research on financial wellbeing.

Limitations and Critique

The model presented in this chapter, together with the research on the predictors of financial wellbeing, is subject to several limitations. Key critiques include:

- **Model limitations:** The model proposed in this chapter has several limitations. At present, it remains a theoretical framework. Although aspects of its structure are supported by existing research, the model in its entirety has not yet been subjected to empirical testing. Moreover, no existing measure currently captures all of its components in a comprehensive manner. From an applied perspective, the model has also not yet been evaluated in practice, and further work is required to develop and test interventions tailored to each of its tiers.
- **Gaps in the literature:** Several sections of the review pointed to a sparse evidence base. More concerningly, some potentially important predictors of financial wellbeing remain unstudied. Examples include contextual country-level factors (economic development, employment rates, social stratification and technological progress), personality dispositions and outlooks (such as self-esteem, values, morality, grit, perfectionism, egoism and altruism, financial stereotypes, frugality and loss aversion), financial needs, goals and decisions, social influence in its various forms, socially responsible financial behaviour, or financial crime. With regard to behaviours, there is a dearth of research on non-traditional employment pathways, career trajectories, or aspects of work (such as job satisfaction) in relation to financial wellbeing. Research on the association between wealth and financial wellbeing is also limited. Further, little is known about how different income sources (investments, dividends, royalties, kinship support or other) relate to financial wellbeing. Evidence is similarly scarce regarding consumption patterns, and there is no research on estate planning. Similarly, no studies have examined the links between ethical financial behaviours and financial wellbeing.
- **Inconsistent findings:** The review highlights inconsistencies across studies in several sections. These discrepancies may stem from the use of varied measurement tools or from differences in national contexts in which the studies were conducted.
- **Cultural differences:** The review includes studies from a range of countries and cultural contexts and deliberately seeks to minimise Western bias by incorporating evidence from other regions. Nevertheless, research on financial wellbeing remains dominated by studies conducted in the West.
- **Causality issues:** Establishing causality is challenging, and most studies reviewed in this chapter have not demonstrated this causal link.
- **Cross-sectional study designs:** Most studies rely on cross-sectional data, providing only a single-time snapshot and limiting insight into how financial wellbeing changes over time.

- **Mediation:** Much of the research reviewed here suggests that the effects of certain factors on financial wellbeing may operate indirectly through mediating variables. Mediation analysis is useful for clarifying these pathways, yet only a small number of the studies cited here employed this approach.
- **Measurement variability:** Within each section, researchers have used a wide range of measures for the same concept. This inconsistency in measurement approaches hampers the interpretation of findings and undermines the capacity to compare findings across studies.
- **Generalisability issues:** Several concepts and strands of empirical research appear to face challenges of generalisability due to methodological issues mentioned above.

Overall, although the existing literature offers useful insights into the predictors of financial wellbeing, it remains fragmented, uneven and methodologically limited. Taken together, these limitations suggest that the field is still in a relatively early stage of development and would benefit from more theoretically integrated, culturally diverse, longitudinal and methodologically rigorous research.

Conclusion

This chapter proposed a novel, applied model of financial wellbeing grounded in the principles of Positive Economic Psychology. In doing so, it sought to address an important gap in the field: the lack of integrative, practically oriented frameworks that translate theory and empirical findings into actionable pathways for improving financial wellbeing. The model conceptualises financial wellbeing as a dynamic process involving psychological dispositions, financial capabilities, decision-making, social context, behaviour and accomplishments. In this sense, the model offers both a conceptual map of the construct and a practical guide for fostering it.

A central contribution of the model is its insistence that financial wellbeing begins with personal dispositions rather than with financial literacy. By positioning dispositions and outlooks as the foundational tier, the model emphasises that traits and attitudes shape whether knowledge is acquired, decisions are made effectively and behaviours are judicious and sustained over time. At the same time, the model recognises that individuals do not operate in a vacuum. Contextual and sociodemographic conditions influence every stage of the process, even if they do not fully determine outcomes. This creates a more balanced account of financial wellbeing, one that acknowledges both personal agency and structural constraint.

The evidence reviewed in this chapter provides encouraging support for the model's main components, while also revealing important limitations in the current literature. Across the different sections, the findings suggest that financial wellbeing is shaped by a complex interplay of internal dispositions, financial capabilities, planning and decisions, social influences, behaviours and objective financial circumstances. Yet the review also showed that the field remains fragmented, with important gaps, inconsistent findings, cultural imbalances and methodological weaknesses. These limitations identify missing areas and guide future research, intervention design and policy development.

Overall, the Pathways Model offers a hopeful yet realistic account of financial wellbeing. It presents financial wellbeing as an attainable, evolving state that can be strengthened through awareness, learning, planning, socially situated action and sustained behavioural habit building, while remaining responsive to life circumstances and economic realities. For practitioners, the model offers a structured tool for assessment and intervention; for individuals and households, it provides a practical roadmap for reflection and action; and for researchers, it offers a foundation for further theoretical refinement and empirical testing. Financial wellbeing, from this perspective, is about developing the psychological, behavioural and social capacities to live well in the financial domain.

8 The Downstream Effects of Financial Wellbeing

Financial wellbeing is increasingly recognised not only as an important outcome in its own right, but also as a factor with wide-ranging consequences across multiple domains of life. While much of the existing literature has focused on the predictors of financial wellbeing, growing attention is now being paid to its downstream effects on psychological functioning, physical health, close relationships, work and subsequent financial outcomes. This broader perspective is important since financial wellbeing shapes how individuals think, feel, relate to others, function in everyday roles and manage future financial demands and opportunities.

At the same time, the evidence base in this area remains uneven. Research directly examining the consequences of financial wellbeing is relatively scarce, with a much larger body of literature focusing on the downstream effects of financial stress or hardship. As a result, this chapter necessarily draws at times on adjacent literatures to shed light on the likely effects of poor financial wellbeing.

This chapter commences by examining the health effects of financial wellbeing (or lack of), and then examines its impact on psychological states. Next, the chapter describes the effects of financial wellbeing on relationships and on work. The chapter concludes by examining the evidence on the ways in which financial wellbeing may affect financial conduct.

HEALTH OUTCOMES

The extant research is limited and indicates that financial wellbeing aligns with positive health status (Netemeyer et al., 2018), whereas financial stress is detrimental, with high financial stress relating to poorer health (Sweet et al., 2013).

To understand how financial strain translates into physical ill-health, the concept of allostatic load provides an important explanatory scaffold. Originally developed by McEwen and Stellar (1993), the allostatic load model conceptualises the body's adaptive responses to stress as physiologically costly. The body triggers a number of physiological responses to deal with stress, including the production of stress hormones. Prolonged or repeated activation of stress responses can lead to strain on the body – allostatic load

DOI: 10.4324/9781003415176-8

– with disruption of metabolic, cardiovascular and immune systems (French, 2023). When financial stressors are chronic, the regulatory systems that ordinarily restore the body to equilibrium cannot do so effectively. Empirical work has linked financial deprivation to biomarkers of allostatic overload: French (2023) found that financial shocks are associated with elevated blood pressure, weight gain and heightened cholesterol.

The cardiovascular consequences of financial strain represent the most extensively researched domain in this literature (Vaccarino & Bremner, 2024). Swarup et al. (2024) conducted a systematic review and reported that financial stress is a significant predictor of a major cardiac event, including myocardial infarction, stroke or cardiovascular death. The mechanisms linking financial strain to cardiovascular risk are psychological stress and the physiological responses to stress (Vaccarino & Bremner, 2024).

Among unemployed young people, more severe hardship and financial stress corresponded to heightened somatic complaints, notably headaches and stomach aches, and a more rapid health decline than among those with lower financial strain (Rantakeisu et al., 1999).

Financial strain has also been identified as a predictor of sleep disturbances (Hall et al., 2008). The pathways through which financial worry disrupts sleep include cognitive and heightened physiological arousal (often due to rumination), and limited access to resources such as adequate housing and noise insulation (Chessa et al., 2025). Insufficient sleep is associated with impaired immune function, elevated inflammatory markers, increased cardiovascular risk and greater all-cause mortality, creating a feedback loop in which financial stress degrades sleep, and degraded sleep further compromises the physiological resources needed to cope with stress.

Financial stress also affects diet. Materially, financial hardship restricts access to fresh, nutritious foods, pushing consumption towards cheaper, calorically dense and nutritionally poor alternatives. Psychologically, stress depletes the cognitive and self-regulatory resources required for deliberate, health-promoting food choices. Research in university students has demonstrated that high financial stress is associated with lower vegetable, fruit, fibre and calcium intake, and high sugar intake (Du et al., 2021).

The relationship between financial strain and substance use is more nuanced than often assumed. There is evidence both of increased substance use as a coping mechanism under financial stress and of reduced consumption when financial hardship constrains spending (Shaw et al., 2011).

Physical inactivity is also a known consequence of financial stress. Engagement in physical activity is constrained by financial hardship through the inability to afford gym memberships or sports equipment, having limited green spaces or safe walking infrastructure, time poverty and the energy-depleting effects of chronic stress and poor sleep (Algren et al., 2015).

Price et al. (2002) found that the association between financial strain and physical health is mediated by diminished personal control and heightened depression. That is, financial strain elevates depression and a sense of loss of control, which in turn leads to health deterioration.

In a Swedish sample, Hagquist (1998) found that adolescents who worried more about their family's finances rated their own health more poorly than peers who did not.

PSYCHOLOGICAL IMPACTS

A modest body of research on the association between financial wellbeing and psychological states indicates that financial wellbeing is a strong predictor of psychological wellbeing (Netemeyer et al., 2018). Consistent with this, Collins and Urban (2021) reported that higher financial wellbeing tracks with greater happiness across the life course (though the authors noted that this association can be seen as bidirectional).

By contrast, the psychological sequelae of financial stress on mental wellbeing have been documented extensively. Lazarevic et al. (2016) found that high financial stress is associated with lower psychological wellbeing. It is also linked to negative emotional states: anxiety, worry, anger and frustration (Peirce et al., 1994). Several studies (Guan et al., 2022; Ettman et al., 2024) found that financial stress is a strong predictor of depression and anxiety, and in a large Norwegian study, the authors reported on hopelessness as a key outcome of financial stress (Bjorndal et al., 2025).

As a chronic stressor, poverty-related stress impairs coping and depletes cognitive resources (Mayo et al., 2022), thereby impairing stress regulation and increasing vulnerability to mental health problems (Schulz et al., 2012), including alcohol misuse (Peirce et al., 1994).

The mental health consequences of financial strain extend to the most severe end of the spectrum, including suicidal ideation and behaviour (O'Connor & Kirtley, 2017). Elbogen et al. (2020) found that cumulative financial strain predicts suicide attempts. The mechanisms underlying this relationship include hopelessness as a mediating variable.

A key question in this literature concerns causal direction: does financial strain produce poor mental health, or are people with pre-existing mental health difficulties more prone to experience financial hardship? The evidence supports a bidirectional relationship (Sivertsen et al., 2025).

The literature also indicates that the effects of parental financial stress can extend to offspring. Financial stress is linked to elevated depressive symptoms and impulsivity among children (Takeuchi et al., 1991). Similarly, adolescents (particularly boys) who perceive their families as having financial strain report reduced mastery, and this lower mastery is related to greater anxiety and depression (Conger et al., 1999). In another study, Conger et al. (2002) found that family financial pressures predict attention-deficit and behavioural problems in children, with pathways operating via heightened parental depression and subsequent changes in parenting.

IMPACT ON RELATIONSHIPS

Empirical work on financial wellbeing as a predictor of relationship quality is limited. Netemeyer et al. (2018) found that higher financial wellbeing is associated with greater perceived relationship support. In contrast, there is abundant research on financial stress and relationships.

The impact of financial strain on intimate partner relationships is well-documented. Longitudinal studies revealed that economic strain predicts financial disagreements in couples (Archuleta et al., 2011) and lower marital satisfaction (Vinokur et al., 1996). Money-related conflicts are qualitatively distinct from other sources of couple disagreement: research using a diary methodology found that financial disputes are characterised by greater length, repetitiveness, more negative emotions and a greater tendency to remain unresolved than conflicts on other topics (Papp et al., 2009). As such, it has substantial implications for relationship stability. Dew et al. (2012) demonstrated that the frequency of financial disagreements predicted divorce more strongly than disagreements on other common topics, highlighting the particular toxicity of unresolved money conflicts.

Couple communication emerges as a moderating factor: the detrimental effect of financial stress on marital quality is significantly amplified when partners also report poor communication (Kelley et al., 2018).

Financial pressure is also associated with heightened depression in both partners, which in turn triggers more irritable, hostile exchanges (Conger et al., 1994; 2002). Conger et al. (2002) proposed that escalating financial pressures narrow couples' focus to money concerns and perceived uncontrollability, engendering frustration, anger and demoralisation. As depressive affect grows, people disengage from their partners, providing less support and spending more time in conflict and mutual blame. In a study of unemployed couples, Vinokur et al. (1996) found that when the job seeker's partner was depressed, they were less able to provide social support and more likely to engage in undermining behaviours such as criticism and insults. This combination is associated with lower relationship satisfaction, a pattern evident for both men and women.

Financial strain also compromises parenting. Mistry et al. (2002) found that financial strain is linked to poorer parenting – less responsiveness to children's needs, reduced affection and more inconsistent and punitive discipline. These parenting patterns, in turn, are associated with children's behavioural difficulties – higher aggression, greater hyperactivity, more frequent disciplinary incidents and poorer academic performance (Mistry et al., 2002).

In a longitudinal study of adolescents and their parents, Conger et al. (1994) found that financial pressure was linked to heightened parent–child conflict, particularly around money. Adolescents' desire to match peers' consumption clashes with parents' constrained budgets, and this tension spills over into adolescents' behaviour outside the home.

Margolin and Gordis (2004) reported that fathers experiencing financial strain showed a higher potential for child abuse than fathers not under such strain. The risk was amplified when financial and parenting stress co-occurred and when there was interparental aggression.

Beyond the family, financial strain systematically erodes the social relationships that typically buffer individuals against adversity. Kung et al. (2022) found a higher probability of reporting loneliness, social isolation and a lack of social support for men and women with lower economic status, establishing what the authors describe as a "loneliness pathway". The mechanisms linking financial hardship to social withdrawal are multiple and mutually reinforcing. Materially, financial strain restricts participation in social activities. The costs of dining out, travelling and participating in leisure activities place such activities beyond reach, progressively narrowing social worlds. Psychologically, the shame and stigma associated with financial difficulties prompt active withdrawal. Reduced social participation in turn diminishes access to the social support that might otherwise moderate the psychological impact of financial hardship, creating a feedback loop in which economic stress and social isolation amplify each other.

WORK UPSHOTS

There is scarce research on financial wellbeing and work-related outcomes, with the only study (Netemeyer et al., 2018) reporting that higher financial wellbeing is associated with greater job satisfaction. However, the relationship between employees' personal financial strain and their functioning in the workplace represents a growing area of empirical inquiry.

Rosso et al. (2024) conducted a review of research and reported that financial stress interferes in the workplace by lowering employee health, performance and commitment and increasing work-family conflict and deviant behaviours. A central mechanism through which stress affects performance is cognitive depletion, whereby chronic worry about financial matters competes with the attentional resources required for task performance and leads to more errors (Mani et al., 2013). A second major pathway linking personal financial strain to work outcomes is through employee burnout (Cusumano & Warmath, 2026). This spillover mechanism, in which financial stress originating outside the workplace manifests as workplace burnout, is consistent with research on chronic stress, which indicates that it can deplete personal and psychological resources, degrading the capacity for sustained effort, engagement and emotional self-regulation at work. Complementary evidence shows that financial stress predicts higher absenteeism (Kim & Garman, 2003).

Rosso et al. (2024) also reported that financially stressed workers are more inclined to spend more time dealing with financial issues during work hours and searching for another job. However, while financial stress motivates job-seeking, severe financial dependency on current employment can suppress voluntary turnover, trapping workers in jobs where they continue to experience reduced performance, wellbeing and low income (Unguren et al., 2024). This creates a workforce in which financially distressed employees may be simultaneously unlikely to leave and unable to perform optimally – a scenario that represents a substantial but largely invisible cost to organisations.

FINANCIAL OUTCOMES

No research has looked into the downstream effects of financial wellbeing on financial conduct or outcomes. However, there is limited research on financial stress, which indicates that it can precipitate poorer financial behaviours (Achtziger, 2022).

One of the most significant findings in the financial stress literature is that economic hardship does not merely result from poor financial behaviour – it actively impairs the cognitive capacities on which sound financial decision-making depends, thereby creating a self-reinforcing cycle. The foundational theoretical account of this process, provided by Wadsworth et al.'s (2011), poverty-related stress framework, emphasises that financial scarcity taxes cognitive bandwidth – the mental resources available for reasoning, planning and self-regulation – leaving less capacity for tasks unrelated to the immediate financial crisis. Research also reveals that financial stress directly impinges on economic decision-making and self-control, with the scarcity mindset driving decisions that may be detrimental in the long run (Shah et al., 2012; 2018). The stress and emotional toll of deprivation can also give rise to coping behaviours such as emotional spending (Haushofer & Fehr, 2014). This body of research reveals a troubling recursive structure in which financial strain lowers cognitive and behavioural capacities that would otherwise enable individuals to improve their financial situation.

LIMITATIONS AND CRITIQUE

Despite the growing body of research on financial wellbeing and its associations with other areas of life, this literature remains marked by several important limitations:

- **Gaps in the literature:** Evidence on how financial wellbeing shapes other life domains is sparse relative to work on financial stress, with research disproportionately targeting physical and mental health, with far less attention to effects on work and financial behaviours – domains of clear relevance for individuals and policymakers.
- **Causality concerns:** Although causal language is common in this body of literature (effect, impact, influence), most studies are correlational, and as noted, several associations may be bidirectional.
- **Measurement variability:** Within each section, researchers have employed a variety of measures to assess the same construct. This inconsistency in

measurement approaches complicates the interpretation of findings and limits the comparability of results across studies.

Overall, these limitations suggest that the literature on financial wellbeing is still developing and should be interpreted with caution. Addressing gaps in outcome coverage, strengthening causal designs and improving measurement consistency would enhance the robustness and practical value of future research.

CONCLUSION

Financial wellbeing can be understood not only as a desirable outcome, but also as a consequential factor shaping a wide range of life domains. The evidence reviewed in this chapter suggests that financial wellbeing is closely linked to better physical and psychological health, more supportive and stable relationships, more favourable work outcomes and potentially more adaptive financial behaviour. Conversely, financial stress seems to have far-reaching downstream effects, operating through emotional, cognitive, behavioural and relational pathways that can compound disadvantage over time.

The chapter has also shown that the literature remains uneven. Direct evidence on the consequences of financial wellbeing is limited, with much of what is known inferred from adjacent research on financial stress. Moreover, although the evidence strongly suggests meaningful associations, causal claims should be treated cautiously, as many studies rely on correlational designs and some relationships are likely to be reciprocal.

The body of research reviewed here indicates that financial scarcity and unmet needs often set in motion cycles of hardship and stress that manifest in poor functioning across several life domains. Crucially, the direction of influence is frequently bi-directional: financial strain can erode cognitive, physical and psychological functioning, and these in turn further undermine financial activity and outcomes, reinforcing disadvantage.

Future research would benefit from moving beyond a narrow focus on financial stress towards a more systematic examination of financial wellbeing as a multidimensional and consequential construct. Stronger longitudinal and experimental designs, greater conceptual clarity and more consistent measurement would help build a more cumulative understanding of its downstream effects.

For policy and practice, the implications are clear: interventions that strengthen financial wellbeing through income supports, affordable credit and debt remediation, robust safety nets and literacy programmes are likely to deliver benefits for mental health, family functioning and work productivity. Ultimately, investing in financial wellbeing is not a narrow economic fix but a public health intervention. It strengthens minds and bodies, relationships and workplaces, and interrupts the feedback loops that keep disadvantage in motion. When we reduce financial strain, we do more than balance budgets – we restore bandwidth, dignity and the capacity to perform economically. The charge is therefore both practical and moral: to build systems that expand opportunity, so that money worries no longer dictate the limits of a life well lived.

ENDNOTE

As this volume concludes, it highlights a central claim: financial wellbeing is not a rarefied outcome but a disciplined, ethically grounded practice that can be intentionally developed. The pathway model offered in Chapter 7 is best understood as a navigational aid rather than a prescriptive ladder, orienting attention to the cultivation of dispositions, the strengthening of capabilities, purposeful planning, sound decision-making, socially situated judgement and the enactment of consistent behaviours that, over time, consolidate into meaningful accomplishments.

The model recognises that context shapes possibilities without fully determining them. Macroeconomic conditions, institutional arrangements and life events set the constraints within which individuals and households operate, yet informed adjustments, prudent use of resources, nurturing support systems and attention to responsibilities beyond the self can expand room for agency. Equally, it is necessary to acknowledge the behavioural forces that may deflect judgement – heuristics, affective responses and social pressures. Recognising these tendencies is a prerequisite for mitigation: through informed, deliberate decision-making, unhealthy patterns can be curtailed and more sustainable practices cultivated.

In an increasingly complex, information-dense and risk-laden financial environment, characterised by modest earning and saving opportunities, weakened safety nets and longer retirements, greater personal stewardship is required. Coherent plans for earning, saving and investing (particularly for later life) help buffer risk exposure and support resilience, while active management of informational "noise" maintains focus on high-impact choices. The cornerstone of progress is self-awareness, intentional self-development of adaptive dispositions and beliefs and capability development: early establishment of sound habits, which create compounding benefits over time. Each tier of the pathway should be approached as a locus for iterative improvement. Modest, repeatable refinements can yield cumulative gains in security, flexibility and preparedness.

Success, accordingly, should be evaluated not solely by accumulation but by enablement: the restoration of cognitive bandwidth, a stable sense of security, greater scope for choice and the capacity to participate and contribute within families, organisations and communities. Readers are invited to return to this pathway as circumstances evolve, to recalibrate aims and to translate intention into disciplined practice, progressing toward financial lives that are more secure, more autonomous and more generative in their effects. Ultimately, the test of financial wellbeing is not what is amassed but what is enabled. Use the pathway as a method to assess, refine and repeat, so that prosperity is not merely possessed but purposefully enacted.

References

Achtziger, A. (2022). Overspending, debt, and poverty. *Current Opinion in Psychology*, *46*, 101342.

Adam, A. M., Frimpong, S., & Boadu, M. O. (2017). Financial literacy and financial planning: Implication for financial well-being of retirees. *Business and Economic Horizons*, *13*(2), 224–236.

Adelman, L., Middleton, S., & Ashworth, K. (2000). *Employment, poverty and social exclusion: Evidence from the poverty and social exclusion survey of britain* (No. 6). PSE Working Paper.

Adler, N. E., Boyce, T., Chesney, M. A., Folkman, S., & Syme, S. L. (1993). Socioeconomic inequalities in health: No easy solution. *Journal of the American Medical Association*, 269(24), 3140–3145.

Adler, N. E., Epel, E. S., Castellazzo, G., & Ickovics, J. R. (2000). Relationship of subjective and objective social status with psychological and physiological functioning: Preliminary data in healthy White women. *Health Psychology*, 19, 586–592.

Agrawal, S., Sharma, N., Bruni, M. E., & Iazzolino, G. (2023). Happiness economics: Discovering future research trends through a systematic literature review. *Journal of Cleaner Production*, 416, 137860.

Ahuvia, A. (2018). Consumption, income, and happiness. In A. Lewis (Ed.), *The Cambridge handbook of psychology and economic behaviour* (pp. 307–339). Cambridge University Press.

Aknin, L. B., Dunn, E. W., & Norton, M. I. (2012). Happiness runs in a circular motion: Evidence for a positive feedback loop between prosocial spending and happiness. *Journal of Happiness Studies*, *13*(2), 347–355.

Aldana, S. G., & Liljenquist, W. (1998). Validity and reliability of a financial strain survey. *Journal of Financial Counseling and Planning*, *9*(2), 11–19.

Algren, M. H., Bak, C. K., Berg-Beckhoff, G., & Andersen, P.T. (2015). Health-risk behaviour in deprived neighbourhoods compared with non-deprived neighbourhoods: A systematic literature review of quantitative observational studies. *PLoS One*, *10*(10), e0139297.

Ameriks, J., Caplin, A., & Leahy, J. (2003). Wealth accumulation and the propensity to plan. *The Quarterly Journal of Economics*, *118*(3), 1007–1047.

Anand, S., & Sen, A. (1994). *Human development index: Methodology and measurement*. Human Development Report Office (HDRO), United Nations Development Programme (UNDP).

Anderloni, L., Bacchiocchi, E., & Vandone, D. (2012). Household financial vulnerability: An empirical analysis. *Research in Economics*, *66*(3), 284–296.

Andraszewicz, S., Kaszás, D., Zeisberger, S., & Holscher, C. (2023). The influence of upward social comparison on retail trading behaviour. *Scientific Reports*, *13*(1), 22713.

Angrisani, M., Barrera, S., Blanco, L. R., & Contreras, S. (2021). The racial/ethnic gap in financial literacy in the population and by income. *Contemporary Economic Policy*, *39*(3), 524–536.

Antonides, G., De Groot, I. M., & van Raaij, W. F. (2011). Mental budgeting and the management of household finance. *Journal of Economic Psychology*, *32*(4), 546–555.

Antonides, G. (2017). Sustainable consumer behaviour: A collection of empirical studies. *Sustainability*, *9*(10), 1686.

Archuleta, K. L., Britt, S. L., Tonn, T. J., & Grable, J. E. (2011). Financial satisfaction and financial stressors in marital satisfaction. *Psychological Reports*, *108*(2), 563–576.

Archuleta, K. L., Grable, J. E., & Britt, S. L. (2013). Financial and relationship satisfaction as a function of harsh start-up and shared goals and values. *Journal of Financial Counseling and Planning*, *24*(1), 3–14.

Ariely, D. (2008). *Predictably irrational*. HarperCollins.

Aristotle. (1255/1984). Politics. In J. Barnes (Ed.), *The complete works of aristotle*. Princeton University Press.

Arkes, H. R., Gigerenzer, G., & Hertwig, R. (2016). How bad is incoherence? *Decision*, *3*(1), 20–39.

Australian Unity. (2021). *20th Anniversary Australian unity wellbeing Index - commemorative report*. Australian Unity and Deakin University.

Babin, B. J., Darden, W. R., & Griffin, M. (1994). Work and/or fun: Measuring hedonic and utilitarian shopping value. *Journal of Consumer Research*, *20*(4), 644–656.

Bai, R. (2023). Impact of financial literacy, mental budgeting and self control on financial wellbeing: Mediating impact of investment decision making. *PLoS One*, *18*(11), e0294466.

Balasuriya, J., Muradoglu, G., & Ayton, P. (2016). *Optimism and portfolio choice*. SSRN.

Ball, R., & Chernova, K. (2008). Absolute income, relative income, and happiness. *Social Indicators Research*, 88, 497–529.

Bannink, F. P., & Geschwind, N. (2021). *Positive CBT*. Hogrefe.

Bannink, F. P., & Peeters, F. (2021). *Practicing positive psychiatry*. Hogrefe.

Bankrate. (2024). *Money and financial stress statistics*. Bankrate.

Barrafrem, K., Tinghög, G., & Västfjäll, D. (2021). Trust in the government increases financial well-being and general well-being during COVID-19. *Journal of Behavioral and Experimental Finance*, *31*, 100514.

Bartosiak, A., Lee, J. E., & Loibl, C. (2025). Fear of missing out, social media influencers, and the social, psychological and financial wellbeing of young consumers. *PLoS One*, 20(4), e0319034.

Baumann, F. (2021). The next frontier—human development and the anthropocene: UNDP human development report 2020. *Environment*, *63*(3), 34–40.

Becker, G. S. (1976). *The economic approach to human behavior*. University of Chicago Press.

Becker, G. S. (1964). *Human capital*. University of Chicago Press.

Behrman, J. R., Mitchell, O. S., Soo, C. K., & Bravo, D. (2012). How financial literacy affects household wealth accumulation. *American Economic Review*, *102*(3), 300–304.

Belk, R. (2018). Ownership: The extended self and the extended object. In J. Peck & S. B. Shu (Eds.), *Psychological ownership and consumer behavior* (pp. 53–67). Springer.

Belsky, G., & Gilovich, T. (2010). *Why smart people make big money mistakes and how to correct them*. Simon and Schuster.

Berlin, M., & Connolly, F. F. (2019). The association between life satisfaction and affective well-being. *Journal of Economic Psychology*, *73*, 34–51.
Berlinger, E., Dobránszky-Bartus, K., & Molnár, G. (2021). Overdue debts and financial exclusion. *Risks*, *9*(9), 158.
Bjorndal, L. D., Roysamb, E., Nes, R. B., von Soest, T., & Ebrahimi, O. V. (2025). Financial factors and depression and anxiety: A symptom-specific approach in the general population. *SSM-Mental Health*, *5*, 100508.
Blanchard, O. (2017). *Macroeconomics* (7th ed.). Pearson.
Boniwell, I., & Tunariu, A. D. (2019). *Positive psychology*. McGraw-Hill Education.
Boyce, C. J., Brown, G. D. A., & Moore, S. C. (2010). Money and happiness: Rank of income, not income, affects life satisfaction. *Psychological Science*, *21*(4), 471–475.
Breitenbach, M., Kapferer, E., Sedmak, C., Breitenbach, M., Kapferer, E., & Sedmak, C. (2021). Stress and poverty: An introduction. In M. Breitenbach, E. Kapferer, & C. Sedmak (Eds.), *Stress and poverty* (pp. 1–19). Springer.
Brisson, D., McCune, S., Wilson, J. H., Speer, S. R., McCrae, J. S., & Hoops Calhoun, K. (2020). A systematic review of the association between poverty and biomarkers of toxic stress. *Journal of Evidence-Based Social Work*, *17*(6), 696–713.
Britt, S. L., Mendiola, M. R., Schink, G. H., Tibbetts, R. H., & Jones, S. H. (2016). Financial stress, coping strategy, and academic achievement of college students. *Journal of Financial Counseling and Planning*, 27(2), 172–183.
Britton, J., Dearden, L., Shephard, N., & Vignoles, A. (2016). *How English domiciled graduate earnings vary with gender, institution attended, subject and socio-economic background* (IFS Working Papers W16/06).
Bronfenbrenner, U. (2005). *Making human beings human*. Sage.
Brown, P. (2017). Education, opportunity and the prospects for social mobility. In P. Brown, D. Reay, & C. Vincent (Eds.), *Education and social mobility* (pp. 60–82). Routledge.
Brown, D. J., Ferris, D. L., Heller, D., & Keeping, L. M. (2007). Antecedents and consequences of the frequency of upward and downward social comparisons at work. *Organizational Behavior and Human Decision Processes*, *102*(1), 59–75.
Brown, J. T., Noone, J., & Salignac, F. (2024). Systems thinking for better social policy: A case study in financial wellbeing. *Journal of Social Policy*, 54(4), 1–17.
Brown, N. J. L., Lomas, T., & Eiroa-Orosa, F. J. (2017). Introduction. In N. J. L. Brown, T. Lomas, & F. J. Eiroa-Orosa (Eds.), *The Routledge international handbook of critical positive psychology* (pp. 1–2). Routledge.
Brown, S., & Gray, D. (2016). Household finances and well-being in Australia: An empirical analysis of comparison effects. *Journal of Economic Psychology*, *53*, 17–36.
Bruggen, E. C., Hogreve, J., Holmlund, M., Kabadayi, S., & Löfgren, M. (2017). Financial well-being: A conceptualization and research agenda. *Journal of Business Research*, *79*, 228–237.
Bullock, H. E. (2019). Psychology's contributions to understanding and alleviating poverty and economic inequality: Introduction to the special section. *American Psychologist*, 74(6), 635–640.
BEA. (2023). *Concepts and methods of the U.S. National income and product accounts*. US Dept of Economics, Bureau of Economic Analysis.
Burke, J., Dunne, P. J., Meehan, T., & O'Boyle, C. (2022). *Positive health*. Routledge.
Burnett, S. (2011). *The happiness Agenda: A modern obsession*. Springer.
Cagetti, M. (2003). Wealth accumulation over the life cycle and precautionary savings. *Journal of Business & Economic Statistics*, *21*(3), 339–353.

Cao, X. J., Xu, Z., & Douma, F. (2012). The interactions between e-shopping and traditional in-store shopping: An application of structural equations model. *Transportation*, *39*(5), 957–974.

Cantril, H. (1965). *The pattern of human concerns*. Rutgers University Press.

Carr, A. (2022). *Positive psychology*. Routledge.

Cartwright, E. (2011). *Behavioral economics*. Routledge.

Carver, C. S., & Scheier, M. F. (2001). Optimism, pessimism, and self-regulation. In E. C. Chang (Ed.), *Optimism & pessimism: Implications for theory, research, and practice* (pp. 31–51). American Psychological Association.

Caso, N., Carling, J., Czaika, M., & Hagen-Zanker, J. (2025). How economic inequalities shape international migration aspirations: A multilevel analysis of perceptions and context. *Population, Space and Place*, *31*(5), e70061.

Castro, D., & Bleys, B. (2023). Do people think they have enough? A subjective income sufficiency assessment. *Ecological Economics*, *205*, 107718.

Castro-González, S., Fernandez-López, S., Rey-Ares, L., & Rodeiro-Pazos, D. (2020). The influence of attitude to money on individuals' financial well-being. *Social Indicators Research*, *148*, 747–764.

CFPB. (2017). *Financial well-being in America*. Consumer Financial Protection Bureau.

CFPB. (2015a). *Financial well-being: The goal of financial education*. Consumer Financial Protection Bureau.

CFPB. (2015b). *Measuring financial well-being*. Consumer Financial Protection Bureau.

Chaulk, B., Johnson, P. J., & Bulcroft, R. (2003). Effects of marriage and children on financial risk tolerance: A synthesis of family development and prospect theory. *Journal of Family and Economic Issues*, *24*, 257–279.

Chen, J., Tang, T. L. P., & Tang, N. (2014). Temptation, monetary intelligence (love of money), and environmental context on unethical intentions and cheating. *Journal of Business Ethics*, *123*, 197–219.

Chen, H., & Volpe, R. P. (2002). Gender differences in personal financial literacy among college students. *Financial Services Review*, *11*(3), 289–307.

Chen, L., & Cao, Q. (2020). Poverty increases the risk of incident cognitive impairment among older adults: a longitudinal study in China. *Aging & Mental Health*, *24*(11), 1822–1827.

Chessa, A., Schrempft, S., Richard, V., Baysson, H., Pullen, N., Zaballa, M.E., Lorthe, E., Nehme, M., Guessous, I, Stringhini, S., & Specchio Study Group. (2025). Perceived financial hardship and sleep in an adult population-based cohort: The mediating role of psychosocial and lifestyle-related factors. *Sleep Health*, *11*(2), 222–229.

Chou, H. T. G., & Edge, N. (2012). "They are happier and having better lives than I am": The impact of using Facebook on perceptions of others' lives. *Cyberpsychology, Behavior, and Social Networking*, *15*(2), 117–121.

Chowdhury, F., & Swaminathan, S. (2024). Does reference-group comparison impact compensatory consumption for bottom of the pyramid (BOP) consumers?. *Journal of Marketing Theory and Practice*, *32*(4), 463–485.

Chujan, W., Ngoc, N. L. B., & Faizi, A. S. (2022). Locus of control on financial Behavior and financial risk attitude. *Annals of Economics & Finance*, *23*(2), 289–313.

Coats, J., & Bajtelsmit, V. L. (2024). New insights into improving financial well-being (Wharton Pension Research Council Working Paper No. WP2024–8, p. 208). TIAA Institute, Research Dialogue.

Coats, J., & Bajtelsmit, V. L. (2021). Optimism, overconfidence, and insurance decisions. *Financial Services Review*, *29*(1), 1–28.

Collins, J. M., & Urban, C. (2021). Measuring financial well-being over the lifecourse. In J. O. S. Wilson, G. A. Panos, & C. Adcock (Eds.), *Financial literacy and responsible finance in the FinTech era* (pp. 45–63). Routledge.

Comerton-Forde, C., De New, J., Salamanca, N., Ribar, D. C., Nicastro, A., & Ross, J. (2022). Measuring financial wellbeing with self-reported and bank record data. *Economic Record*, *98*(321), 133–151.

Comerton-Forde, C., Ip, E., Ribar, D.C., Ross, J., Salamanca, N., & Tsiaplias, S. (2018). *Using survey and banking data to measure financial wellbeing*. Commonwealth Bank of Australia and Melbourne Institute Financial Well-being Scales Technical Report, 1.

Compton, W. C., & Hoffman, E. (2019). *Positive psychology*. Sage.

Conger, R. D., Ge, X., Elder Jr, G. H., Lorenz, F. O., & Simons, R. L. (1994). Economic stress, coercive family process, and developmental problems of adolescents. *Child Development*, *65*(2), 541–561.

Conger, R. D., Reuter, M. A., & Elder, G. H. (1999). Couple resilience to economic pressure. *Journal of Personality and Social Psychology*, *76*, 54–71.

Conger, R. D., Wallace, L. E., Sun, Y., Simons, R. L., McLoyd, V. C., & Brody, G. H. (2002). Economic pressure in African American families: A replication and extension of the family stress model. *Developmental Psychology*, *38*(2), 179.

Cooper, K. (2021). Are poor parents poor parents? The relationship between poverty and parenting among mothers in the UK. *Sociology*, *55*(2), 349–383.

Cowell, F. A. (2011). *Measuring inequality*. Oxford University Press.

Creamer, J., Shrider, E. A., Burns, K., & Chen, F. (2022). *Poverty in the United States: 2021*. US Census Bureau.

Cusumano, C., & Warmath, D. (2026). Mind the gap: Investigating how financial well-being shapes job satisfaction through burnout. *Journal of Workplace Behavioral Health*, *41*(1), 189–203.

D'Ambrosio, C., Jäntti, M., & Lepinteur, A. (2020). Money and happiness: Income, wealth and subjective well-being. *Social Indicators Research*, *148*(1), 47–66.

Danese, A., & McEwen, B. S. (2012). Adverse childhood experiences, allostasis, allostatic load, and age-related disease. *Physiology & Behavior*, *106*(1), 29–39.

Dangol, J., & Maharjan, S. (2018). Parental and peer influence on the saving behavior of the youth. *The International Research Journal of Management Science*, *3*, 42–63.

Davies, J. B. (2011). *Personal wealth from a global perspective*. Oxford University Press.

De Almeida, F., Ferreira, M. B., Soro, J. C., & Silva, C. S. (2021). Attitudes toward money and control strategies of financial behavior: A comparison between overindebted and non-overindebted consumers. *Frontiers in Psychology*, *12*, 566594.

De Bruijn, E. J., & Antonides, G. (2020). Determinants of financial worry and rumination. *Journal of Economic Psychology*, *76*, 102233.

Deci, E. L., & Ryan, R. M. (2008). Hedonia, eudaimonia, and well-being: An introduction. *Journal of Happiness Studies*, *9*(1), 1–11.

Deci, E. L., & Ryan, R. M. (2000). The "what" and "why" of goal pursuits: Human needs and the self-determination of behavior. *Psychological Inquiry*, *11*(4), 227–268.

Delistavrou, A., & Tilikidou, I. (2012). Exploring the ethical behaviour adopted by greek consumers. *Journal of Marketing Vistas*, *1*(2), 22–35.

Demirguc-Kunt, A., Klapper, L., Singer, D., Ansar, S., & Hess, J. (2018). *The global findex database 2017*. World Bank Publications.

DeNavas-Walt, C., Proctor, B. D., & Smith, J. C. (2013). *Income, poverty, and health insurance coverage in the United States: 2012*. U.S. Census Bureau, Current Population Reports.

De Vries, R. (2014). *Earning by degrees. Sutton trust report*. The Sutton Trust.

Dew, J., Britt, S., & Huston, S. (2012). Examining the relationship between financial issues and divorce. *Family Relations*, *61*(4), 615–628.

Dhiman, N., & Kumar, A. (2023). What we know and don't know about consumer happiness: Three-decade review, synthesis, and research propositions. *Journal of Interactive Marketing*, *58*(2–3), 115–135.

Diener, E. (2000). Subjective well-being: The science of happiness and a proposal for a national index. *American Psychologist*, *55*(1), 34–43.

Diener, E., Emmons, R. A., Larsen, R. J., & Griffin, S. (1985). The satisfaction with life scale. *Journal of Personality Assessment*, *49*(1), 71–75.

Diener, E., Lucas, R. E., & Oishi, S. (2018). Advances and open questions in the science of subjective well-being. *Collabra: Psychology*, *4*(1), 15.

Diener, E., Suh, E. M., Lucas, R. E., & Smith, H. L. (1999). Subjective well-being: Three decades of progress. *Psychological Bulletin*, *125*(2), 276.

Diener, E., Wirtz, D., Tov, W., Kim-Prieto, C., Choi, D. W., Oishi, S., & Biswas-Diener, R. (2010). New well-being measures: Short scales to assess flourishing and positive and negative feelings. *Social Indicators Research*, *97*, 143–156.

Donaldson, S. I., van Zyl, L. E., & Donaldson, S. I. (2022). PERMA+ 4: A framework for work-related wellbeing, performance and positive organizational psychology 2.0. *Frontiers in Psychology*, *12*, 817244.

Dong, J., Smieliauskas, F., & Konetzka, R.T. (2019). Effects of long-term care insurance on financial well-being. *Geneva Papers on Risk and Insurance: Issues and Practice*, *44*(2), 277–302.

Donnelly, G., Iyer, R., & Howell, R.T. (2012). The Big Five personality traits, material values, and financial well-being of self-described money managers. *Journal of Economic Psychology*, *33*(6), 1129–1142.

Drechsel-Grau, M., & Greimel, F. (2024). *Falling behind: Has rising inequality fueled the American debt boom?* (No. 11565). CESifo Working Paper.

Du, C., Wang, W., Hsiao, P. Y., Ludy, M. J., & Tucker, R. M. (2021). Insufficient sleep and poor sleep quality completely mediate the relationship between financial stress and dietary risk among higher education students. *Behavioral Sciences*, *11*(5), 69.

Duncan, G. J., & Magnuson, K. (2012). Socioeconomic status and cognitive functioning: Moving from correlation to causation. *Cognitive Science*, *3*(3), 377–386.

Dwyer, R. E., McCloud, L., & Hodson, R. (2012). Debt and graduation from American universities. *Social Forces*, *90*(4), 1133–1155.

Easterbrook, M. J. (2021). *The social psychology of economic inequality*. The United Nations University World Institute for Development Economics Research (UNU-WIDER Working Paper No. 2021/43).

Easterlin, R. A. (2004). The economics of happiness. *Daedalus*, *133*(2), 26–33.

Elbogen, E. B., Lanier, M., Montgomery, A. E., Strickland, S., Wagner, H. R., & Tsai, J. (2020). Financial strain and suicide attempts in a nationally representative sample of US adults. *American Journal of Epidemiology*, *189*(11), 1266–1274.

Elliott, M. V., Johnson, S. L., Pearlstein, J. G., Lopez, D. E. M., & Keren, H. (2023). Emotion-related impulsivity and risky decision-making: A systematic review and meta-regression. *Clinical Psychology Review*, *100*, 102232.

Ettman, C. K., Fan, A. ., Philips, A. P., Adam, G. P., Ringlein, G., Clark, M. A., Wilson, I. B., Vivier, P. M., & Galea, S. (2023). Financial strain and depression in the US: A scoping review. *Translational Psychiatry*, *13*(1), 168.

Ettman, C. K., Thornburg, B., Abdalla, S. M., Meiselbach, M. K., & Galea, S. (2024). Financial assets and mental health over time. *Scientific Reports*, *14*(1), 27370.

Evans, J., Cross, K. A., & Collard, S. B. (2024). *Bumpy road to recovery: The financial wellbeing of UK households in May 2024: Findings from the 10th financial fairness tracker survey*. University of Bristol Personal Finance Research Centre.

Faber, J. W. (2019). Segregation and the cost of money: Race, poverty, and the prevalence of alternative financial institutions. *Social Forces*, *98*(2), 819–848.

Fan, L., & Henager, R. (2022). A structural determinants framework for financial well-being. *Journal of Family and Economic Issues*, *43*(2), 415–428.

Fan, L., & Park, N. (2021). Factors mediating the association between financial socialization and well-being of young adults: testing a conceptual framework. *Journal of Financial Counseling and Planning*, *32*(2), 202–216.

Farrag, D. A., El Sayed, I. M., & Belk, R. W. (2010). Mall shopping motives and activities: A multimethod approach. *Journal of International Consumer Marketing*, *22*(2), 95–115.

Fenton-O'Creevy, M., & Furnham, A. (2022). Money attitudes, financial capabilities, and impulsiveness as predictors of wealth accumulation. *PLoS One*, *17*(11), e0278047.

Fenton-O'Creevy, M., & Furnham, A. (2020a). Money attitudes, personality and chronic impulse buying. *Applied Psychology*, *69*(4), 1557–1572.

Fenton-O'Creevy, M., & Furnham, A. (2020b). Personality, ideology, and money attitudes as correlates of financial literacy and competence. *Financial Planning Review*, *3*(1), e1070.

Fenton-O'Creevy, M., Dibb, S., & Furnham, A. (2018). Antecedents and consequences of chronic impulsive buying: Can impulsive buying be understood as dysfunctional self-regulation?. *Psychology & Marketing*, *35*(3), 175–188.

Fernandes, D., Lynch, J. G., Jr, & Netemeyer, R. G. (2014). Financial literacy, financial education, and downstream financial behaviors. *Management Science*, *60*(8), 1861–1883.

Festinger, L. (1954). A theory of social comparison processes. *Human Relations*, *7*(2), 117–140.

Fidelity. (2024). *Global financial wellness survey*. Fidelity.

Filep, S., Laing, J., & Csikszentmihalyi, M. (2016). What is positive tourism? Why do we need it? In S. Filep, J. Laing, & M. Csikszentmihalyi (Eds.), *Positive tourism* (pp. 17–30). Routledge.

FCA. (2023). *Financial lives: 2023 survey*. Financial Conduct Authority.

Flik, R. J., & Van Praag, B. M. (1991). Subjective poverty line definitions. *De Economist*, *139*(3), 311–330.

Forgeard, M. J. C., Jayawickreme, E., Kern, M., & Seligman, M. E. P. (2011). Doing the right thing: Measuring wellbeing for public policy. *International Journal of Wellbeing*, *1*(1), 79–106.

Forgeard, M. J., & Seligman, M. E. P. (2012). Seeing the glass half full: A review of the causes and consequences of optimism. *Pratiques Psychologiques*, *18*(2), 107–120.

Frankham, C., Richardson, T., & Maguire, N. (2020). Do locus of control, self-esteem, hope and shame mediate the relationship between financial hardship and mental health? *Community Mental Health Journal*, *56*(3), 404–415.

French, D. (2023). From financial wealth shocks to ill-health: Allostatic load and overload. *Health Economics*, *32*(4), 939–952.

French, D., & Vigne, S. (2019). The causes and consequences of household financial strain: A systematic review. *International Review of Financial Analysis*, *62*, 150–156.

Friedline, T., Chen, Z., & Morrow, S.P. (2021). Families' financial stress and well-being: The importance of the economy and economic environments. *Journal of Family and Economic Issues*, *42*, 34–51.

Frijters, P., Clark, A. E., Krekel, C., & Layard, R. (2020). A happy choice: Wellbeing as the goal of government. *Behavioural Public Policy*, *4*(2), 126–165.

FRS. (2023). *Economic well-being of U.S. Households in 2022*. The USA Federal Reserve System.

Fu, J. (2020). Ability or opportunity to act: What shapes financial well-being? *World Development*, *128*, 104843.

Fudenberg, D. (2006). Advancing beyond advances in behavioural economics. *Journal of Economic Literature*, *44*(3), 694–711.

Furnham, A., & Cheng, H. (2017). Socio-demographic indicators, intelligence, and locus of control as predictors of adult financial well-being. *Journal of Intelligence*, *5*(2), 11.

Furnham, A., Wilson, E., & Telford, K. (2012). The meaning of money: The validation of a short money-types measure. *Personality and Individual Differences*, *52*, 707–711.

Furreboe, E. F., & Nyhus, E. K. (2022). Financial self-efficacy, financial literacy, and gender: A review. *Journal of Consumer Affairs*, *56*(2), 743–765.

Gable, S. L., & Haidt, J. (2005). What (and why) is positive psychology? *Review of General Psychology*, *9*(2), 103–110.

Gajos, J. M., Totenhagen, C.J., & Wilmarth, M.J. (2022). The association between financial strain and volatility in daily relationship uncertainty: A dyadic investigation. *Journal of Social and Personal Relationships*, *39*(5), 1412–1433.

Galbraith, J. K. (1938). Rational and irrational consumer preference. *The Economic Journal*, *48*(190), 336–342.

Gallup. (2024). *Global life evaluation Index*. Gallup.

Gallup. (2014). *State of global well-being*. Gallup.

Gallie, D., & Paugam, S. (2000). The experience of unemployment in Europe: The debate. *Age*, 15(24), 12–9.

Garcia, S. M., Tor, A., & Schiff, T.M. (2013). The psychology of competition: A social comparison perspective. *Perspectives on Psychological Science*, *8*(6), 634–650.

Garcia-Castro, J. D., Willis, G. B., & Rodríguez-Bailón, R. (2019). I know people who can and who cannot: A measure of the perception of economic inequality in everyday life. *The Social Science Journal*, *56*(4), 599–608.

Garcia-Mata, O., & Zeron-Felix, M. (2022). A review of the theoretical foundations of financial well-being. *International Review of Economics*, *69*(2), 145–176.

Garcia-Mata, O., Zerón-Félix, M., & Briano, G. (2022). Financial well-being index in Mexico. *Social Indicators Research*, *163*(1), 111–135.

Gardarsdottir, R. B., & Dittmar, H. (2012). The relationship of materialism to debt and financial wellbeing: the case of Iceland's perceived prosperity. *Journal of Economic Psychology*, *33*, 471–481.

Gasiorowska, A. (2014). The relationship between objective and subjective wealth is moderated by financial control and mediated by money anxiety. *Journal of Economic Psychology*, *43*, 64–74.

Gathergood, J., & Weber, J. (2017). Financial literacy, present bias and alternative mortgage products. *Journal of Banking & Finance*, *78*, 58–83.

Gedara, N. I. M. (2021). The men's marriage premium in the United States: What remains after controlling for publication bias and heterogeneity?. *Colombo Business Journal*, *12*(2), 53–79.

Gerardi, K. (2010). *Financial literacy and subprime mortgage delinquency*. Diane Publishing.

Gigerenzer, G. (2018). The bias bias in behavioral economics. *Review of Behavioral Economics*, *5*(3–4), 303–336.
Gigerenzer, G. (2015). *Simply rational.* Oxford University Press.
Gignac, G.E. (2022). The association between objective and subjective financial literacy: Failure to observe the Dunning-Kruger effect. *Personality and Individual Differences*, *184*, 111224.
Gilovich, T., Griffin, D., & Kahneman, D. (Eds.). (2002). *Heuristics and biases.* Cambridge University Press.
Gilroy, H., Nava, A., Maddoux, J., McFarlane, J., Symes, L., Koci, A., & Fredland, N. (2015). Poverty, partner abuse, and women's mental health: New knowledge for better practice. *Journal of Social Service Research*, *41*(2), 145–157.
Girshina, A. (2019). *Wealth, savings, and returns over the life cycle: The role of education.* Swedish House of Finance Research Paper, 19–10.
Gladstone, J. J., & Pomerance, J. (2025). A glass half full of money: Dispositional optimism and wealth accumulation across the income spectrum. *Journal of Personality and Social Psychology*, *128*(1), 147–195.
Gleitman, H., Gross, J., & Reisberg, D. (2011). *Psychology*. Norton & Company.
Goncalves, V. N., Ponchio, M. C., & Basílio, R. G. (2021). Women's financial well-being: A systematic literature review and directions for future research. *International Journal of Consumer Studies*, *45*(4), 824–843.
Goodman, F., Disabato, D., Kashdan, T., & Kauffman, S. (2017). Measuring well-being: A comparison of subjective wellbeing and PERMA. *The Journal of Positive Psychology*, 13(4), 1–12.
Goyal, K., Kumar, S., & Xiao, J. J. (2021). Antecedents and consequences of personal financial management behavior: A systematic literature review and future research agenda. *International Journal of Bank Marketing*, *39*(7), 1166–1207.
Grable, J. E, Heo, W., & Rabbani, A. (2015). Financial anxiety, physiological arousal, and planning intention. *Journal of Financial Therapy*, *5*(2), 2.
Grable, J. E., & Joo, S. (2004). Environmental and bio psychosocial factors associated with financial risk tolerance. *Financial Counseling and Planning*, *15*(1), 73–82.
Grevenbrock, N. (2020). Dispositional optimism (and pessimism), wealth, and stock market participation. *Journal of Economic Psychology*, *81*, 102328.
Greene, J. D., & Seligman, M. E. P. (Eds.). (2016). *Positive neuroscience.* Oxford University Press.
Green, S., & Palmer, S. (Eds.). (2018). *Positive psychology coaching in practice.* Routledge.
Grinstein-Weiss, M., Yeo, Y. H., Zhan, M., & Charles, P. (2008). Asset holding and net worth among households with children: Differences by household type. *Children and Youth Services Review*, *30*(1), 62–78.
Grohmann, A. (2016). The gender gap in financial literacy: Income, education, and experience offer only partial explanations. *DIW Economic Bulletin*, *6*(46/47), 531–537.
Grohmann, A., Kluhs, T., & Menkhoff, L. (2018). Does financial literacy improve financial inclusion? Cross country evidence. *World Development*, *111*, 84–96.
Guan, N., Guariglia, A., Moore, P., Xu, F., & Al-Janabi, H. (2022). Financial stress and depression in adults: A systematic review. *PLoS One*, *17*(2), e0264041.
Gudmunson, C. G., & Danes, S. M. (2011). Family financial socialization: Theory and critical review. *Journal of Family and Economic Issues*, *32*(4), 644–667.
Guo, B., & Huang, J. (2023). Financial well-being and financial capability among low-income entrepreneurs. *Journal of Risk and Financial Management*, *16*(3), 181.
Gupta, A., Mishra, S., Behera, D. K., & Abhilash, A. (2025). Harnessing financial advice and literacy for financial well-being in the digital age. *Investment Management and Financial Innovations*, *22*(1), 299.

Guthrie, L. C., Butler, S. C., & Ward, M. M. (2009). Time perspective and socioeconomic status: A link to socioeconomic disparities in health?. *Social Science & Medicine*, *68*(12), 2145–2151.

Gutter, M. S, & Copur, Z. (2011). Financial behaviors and financial well-being of college students: Evidence from a national survey. *Journal of Family and Economic Issues*, *32*(4), 699–714.

Gutter, M. S., Copur, Z., & Blanco, A. (2014). Racial differences in financial socialization and financial behaviors of US college students. In H. Dinçer (Ed.), *Global strategies in banking and finance* (pp. 272–292). IGI Global.

Hagquist, C.E. (1998). Economic stress and perceived health among adolescents in Sweden. *Journal of Adolescent Health, 22*(3), 250–257.

Haisken-DeNew, J., Ribar, D. C., Salamanca, N., & Nicastro, A. (2018). *Using survey and banking data to understand Australians' financial wellbeing*. Commonwealth Bank of Australia and Melbourne Institute Financial Wellbeing Scales Technical Report, 2.

Hall, M., Buysse, D. J., Nofzinger, E. A., Reynolds III, C. F., Thompson, W., Mazumdar, S., & Monk, T. H. (2008). Financial strain is a significant correlate of sleep continuity disturbances in late-life. *Biological Psychology*, *77*(2), 217–222.

Hansen, M. N. (2014). Self-made wealth or family wealth? Changes in intergenerational wealth mobility. *Social Forces*, *93*(2), 457–481.

Hart, R. (2020). *Positive psychology: The basics*. Routledge.

Hart, R., & Hart, D. (2026). Cutting through the clutter: cleaning the lens on work-related wellbeing concept. *Behavioral Sciences*, *16*(3), 373.

Hart, R., & Hart, D. (2025). New frontier: Positive economic psychology. *Open Psychology*, *7*(1), 20250004.

Hashmi, F., Aftab, H., Martins, J. M., Nuno Mata, M., Qureshi, H. A., Abreu, A., & Mata, P. N. (2021). The role of self-esteem, optimism, deliberative thinking and self-control in shaping the financial behavior and financial well-being of young adults. *PLoS One*, *16*(9), e0256649.

Haushofer, J., & Salicath, D. (2023). The psychology of poverty: Where do we stand?. *Social Philosophy and Policy*, *40*(1), 150–184.

Haushofer, J., & Fehr, E. (2014). On the psychology of poverty. *Science*, *344*(6186), 862–867.

Hayajneh, A. A., & Rababa, M. (2022). The association of frailty with poverty in older adults: A systematic review. *Dementia and Geriatric Cognitive Disorders*, *50*(5), 407–413.

Hawkins, B. P., & Zuiker, V. S. (2019). Financial counselors' experiences working with clients of color: Lessons of cultural awareness. *Journal of Financial Counseling and Planning*, *30*(1), 6–17.

Headey, B. (2024). Bottom-up versus top-down theories of life satisfaction. In F. Maggino (Ed.), *Encyclopedia of quality of life and well-being research* (pp. 489–491). Springer

Hefferon, K. (2013). *Positive psychology and the body*. Open University Press.

Henchoz, C., Coste, T., & Wernli, B. (2019). Culture, money attitudes and economic outcomes. *Swiss Journal of Economics and Statistics*, *155*(2), 1–13.

Henderson, L., & Knight, T. (2012). Integrating the hedonic and eudaimonic perspectives to more comprehensively understand wellbeing and pathways to wellbeing. *International Journal of Wellbeing*, *2*(3), 196–221.

Henrich, J., Heine, S.J., & Norenzayan, A. (2010). The weirdest people in the world? *Behavioral and Brain Sciences*, *33*(2–3), 61–135.

Hebert, S., & Gyarmati, D. (2014). *Financial capability and essential skills: An exploratory analysis*. Social Research and Demonstration Corporation.

Hershey, D. A., Jacobs-Lawson, J. M., McArdle, J. J., & Hamagami, F. (2007). Psychological foundations of financial planning for retirement. *Journal of Adult Development*, *14*(1), 26–36.

Hershfield, H. E., Goldstein, D. G., Sharpe, W. F., Fox, J., Yeykelis, L., Carstensen, L. L., & Bailenson, J. N. (2011). Increasing saving behavior through age-progressed renderings of the future self. *Journal of Marketing Research*, *48*(SPL), S23–S37.

Hertwig, R., & Grune-Yanoff, T. (2021). Boosting and nudging: Two paths toward better financial decisions. In R. Viale, U. Filotto, B. Alemanni, & S. Mousavi (Eds.), *Financial education and risk literacy* (pp. 150–180). Edward Elgar.

Hertwig, R., & Grüne-Yanoff, T. (2017). Nudging and boosting: Steering or empowering good decisions. *Perspectives on Psychological Science*, *12*(6), 973–986.

Hills, P., & Argyle, M. (2002). The Oxford happiness questionnaire: A compact scale for the measurement of psychological well-being. *Personality and Individual Differences*, *33*(7), 1073–1082.

Holmes, J., & Kiernan, K. (2013). Persistent poverty and children's development in the early years of childhood. *Policy & Politics*, *41*(1), 19–42.

Howell, R. T., Pchelin, P., & Iyer, R. (2012). The preference for experiences over possessions: Measurement and construct validation of the experiential buying tendency scale. *The Journal of Positive Psychology*, *7*(1), 57–71.

Howitt, D., & Cramer, D. (2020). *Research methods in psychology*. Pearson.

Howlett, E., Kees, J., & Kemp, E. (2008). The role of self-regulation, future orientation, and financial knowledge in long-term financial decisions. *Journal of Consumer Affairs*, *42*(2), 223–242.

Hubler, D. S., Burr, B. K., Garnder, B. C., Larzelere, R. E., & Busby, D. M. (2015). The intergernational transmission of financial stress and relationship outcomes. *Marriage and Family Review*, *52*(4), 373–391.

Huta, V. (2016). Eudaimonic and hedonic orientations: Theoretical considerations and research findings. In J. Vitterso (Ed.), *Handbook of eudaimonic well-being* (pp. 215–231), Springer.

Huta, V., & Waterman, A. S. (2014). Eudaimonia and its distinction from hedonia: Developing a classification and terminology for understanding conceptual and operational definitions. *Journal of Happiness Studies*, *15*, 1425–1456.

Ianole-Calin, R., Hubona, G., Druica, E., & Basu, C. (2021). Understanding sources of financial well-being in Romania: A prerequisite for transformative financial services. *Journal of Services Marketing*, *35*(2), 152–168.

Ingham, G. (2004). *The nature of money*. Polity Press.

Innes, A.M. (1914). The credit theory of money. *Banking Law Journal*, *31*(2), 151–168.

Iramani, R., & Lutfi, L. (2021). An integrated model of financial well-being: The role of financial behavior. *Accounting*, *7*(3), 691–700.

Jaikumar, S., Sarin, A., Narayanan, P., & Kumari, R. (2025). Effects of income inequality in an emerging economy on subjective economic well-being: Suppressing effect of conspicuous consumption. *Journal of Marketing Theory and Practice*, 1–19.

Jaikumar, S., & Sharma, Y. (2021). Consuming beyond means: Debt trap of conspicuous consumption in an emerging economy. *Journal of Marketing Theory and Practice*, *29*(2), 233–249.

Jansson-Boyd, C. (2019). *Consumer psychology*. McGraw-Hill Education.

Joireman, J., Sprott, D. E., & Spangenberg, E. R. (2005). Fiscal responsibility and the consideration of future consequences. *Personality and Individual Differences*, *39*(6), 1159–1168.

Jolliffe, D., & Prydz, E.B. (2021). Societal poverty: A relative and relevant measure. *The World Bank Economic Review*, *35*(1), 180–206.
Joo, S., & Grable, J. E. (2004). An exploratory framework of the determinants of financial satisfaction. *Journal of Family and Economic Issues*, *25*(1), 25–50.
Jorgensen, B. L., & Savla, J. (2010). Financial literacy of young adults: The importance of parental socialization. *Family Relations*, *59*, 465–478.
Kahneman, D. (2011). *Thinking, fast and slow*. Macmillan.
Kahneman, D., Sibony, O., & Sunstein, C. R. (2021). *Noise*. Hachette.
Kahneman, D., & Tversky, A. (1996). On the reality of cognitive illusions. *Psychological Review*, *103*(3), 582–591.
Kahneman, D., & Tversky, A. (1979). Prospect theory: An analysis of decision under risk. *Econometrica*, *47*(2), 263–291.
Kalinowski, S., & Rosa, A. (2021). Sustainable development and the problems of rural poverty and social exclusion in the EU countries. *European Research Studies Journal*, *XXIV*(2), 438–463.
Kalleberg, A. L. (2011). *Good jobs, bad jobs*. Russell Sage Foundation.
Kamble, P. A., Mehta, A., & Rani, N. (2024). Financial inclusion and digital financial literacy: Do they matter for financial well-being?. *Social Indicators Research*, *171*(3), 777–807.
Kapeller, J., & Schütz, B. (2015). Conspicuous consumption, inequality and debt: the nature of consumption-driven profit-led regimes. *Metroeconomica*, *66*(1), 51–70.
Kasser, T. (2018). Materialism and living well. In E. Diener, S. Oishi, & L. Tay (Eds.), *Handbook of well-being* (pp. 860–871). DEF Publishers.
Katona, G. (1951). *Psychological analysis of economic behavior*. Elsevier.
Kaur, G., Singh, M., & Singh, S. (2021). Mapping the literature on financial well-being: A systematic literature review and bibliometric analysis. *International Social Science Journal*, *71*(241–242), 217–241.
Kelley, H. H., LeBaron, A. B., & Hill, E. J. (2018). Financial stress and marital quality: The moderating influence of couple communication. *Journal of Financial Therapy*, *9*(2), 18–36.
Kelley, T. L. (1927). *Interpretation of educational measurements*. World Book Co.
Kempson, E., Finney, A., & Poppe, C. (2017). Financial well-being: A conceptual model and preliminary analysis. *Consumer Financial Protection Bureau*, Project note 3-2017.
Kern, M. L., & Wehmeyer, M. L. (2021). *The Palgrave handbook of positive education*. Springer Nature.
Keynes, J. M. (1936). *The general theory of employment, interest and money*. Palgrave.
Kim, J., & Garman, E. T. (2003). Financial Stress and absenteeism: An empirically. derived model. *Journal of Financial Counseling and Planning*, *14*(1), 31–42.
Kim, J. E., & Moen, P. (2002). Retirement transitions, gender, and psychological well-being: A life-course, ecological model. *The Journals of Gerontology Series B: Psychological Sciences and Social Sciences*, *57*(3), P212–P222.
Kimball, M.-S., & Willis, R. J. (2023). *Utility and happiness*. National Bureau of Economic Research. Working paper 31707.
Kirchler, E., & Hoelzl, E. (2018). *Economic psychology*. Cambridge University Press.
Kirchler, E., & Hoelzl, E. (2006). Twenty-five years of the *Journal of Economic Psychology* (1981–2005): A report on the development of an interdisciplinary field of research. *Journal of Economic Psychology*, *27*(6), 793–804.
Klapper, L., & Lusardi, A. (2020). Financial literacy and financial resilience: Evidence from around the world. *Financial Management*, *49*(3), 589–614.
Klontz, B. T., & Britt, S. L. (2012). How clients' money scripts predict their financial behaviors. *Journal of Financial Planning*, *25*, 46–53.

Klontz, B., Britt, S. L., Mentzer, J., & Klontz, T. (2011). Money beliefs and financial behaviors: Development of the klontz money script inventory. *Journal of Financial Therapy*, 2(1), 1.

Klontz, B., Chaffin, C. R., & Klontz, T. (2022). *Psychology of financial planning*. Wiley.

Klontz, B. T., Sullivan, P., Seay, M. C., & Canale, A. (2015). The wealthy: A financial psychological profile. *Consulting Psychology Journal: Practice and Research*, *67*(2), 127–143.

Klugman, J., Rodriguez, F., & Choi, H. (2011). The HDI 2010: New controversies, old critiques. *Journal of Economic Inequality*, 9(2), 249–288.

Knabe, A., Ratzel, S., Schob, R., & Weimann, J. (2010). Dissatisfied with life but having a good day: Time-use and well-being of the unemployed. *The Economic Journal*, *120*(547), 867–889.

Kooij, D. T., Kanfer, R., Betts, M., & Rudolph, C. W. (2018). Future time perspective: A systematic review and meta-analysis. *Journal of Applied Psychology*, *103*(8), 867–893.

Koots-Ausmees, L., Realo, A., & Allik, J. (2013). The relationship between life satisfaction and emotional experience in 21 European countries. *Journal of Cross-Cultural Psychology*, 44(2), 223–244.

Kotler, P., & Keller, K. L. (2016). *Marketing management* (15th ed.). Pearson.

Kraus, M. W., Piff, P. K., Mendoza-Denton, R., Rheinschmidt, M. L., & Keltner, D. (2012). Social class, solipsism, and contextualism: How the rich are different from the poor. *Psychological Review*, *119*(3), 546–572.

Krugman, P., & Wells, R. (2018). *Economics* (5th ed.). Worth Publishers.

Kumar, J., Rani, V., Rani, G., & Sarker, T. (2023). Determinants of the financial wellbeing of individuals in an emerging economy: An empirical study. *International Journal of Bank Marketing*, *41*(4), 860–881.

Kung, C. S., Pudney, S. E., & Shields, M. A. (2022). Economic gradients in loneliness, social isolation and social support: Evidence from the UK Biobank. *Social Science & Medicine*, *306*, 115122.

Kursunluoglu, E. (2014). Shopping centre customer service: Creating customer satisfaction and loyalty. *Marketing Intelligence & Planning*, *32*(4), 528–548.

Lamas, S., & Murphy, R.O. (2021). Simple decision-making rules of thumb and financial well-being. *Journal of Personal Finance*, *20*(2), 22–34.

Lambert, M. J. C. M., Jusoh, Z. M., Abd Rahim, H., & Zainudin, N. (2023). Factors affecting financial well-being of millennials: A systematic review. *Information Management and Business Review*, *15*(2), 98–108.

Landefeld, J. S., Seskin, E. P., & Fraumeni, B. M. (2008). Taking the pulse of the economy: Measuring GDP. *Journal of Economic Perspectives*, 22(2), 193–216.

Laurent, G., & Kapferer, J. N. (1985). Measuring consumer involvement profiles. *Journal of Marketing Research*, 22(1), 41–53.

Layard, R., Mayraz, G., & Nickell, S. (2010). Does relative income matter? Are the critics right. In E. Diener, J. F. Helliwell & D. Kahneman (Eds.), *International differences in well-being* (pp. 139–166). Oxford University Press.

Lazarevic, V., Holman, E. G., Oswald, R. F., & Kramer, K. Z. (2016). Relations between economic well-being, family support, community attachment, and life satisfaction among LGBQ adults. *Journal of Family and Economic Issues*, *37*(4), 594–606.

Lazarus, R. S., & Folkman, S. (1984). *Stress: Appraisal and coping*. Springer.

Lea, S. E., Tarpy, R. M., & Webley, P. (1987). *The individual in the economy*. Cambridge University Press.

Lee, J. M., & Kim, K. T. (2016). The role of propensity to plan on retirement savings and asset accumulation. *Family and Consumer Sciences Research Journal*, *45*(1), 34–48.

Lee, J. E., & Watkins, B. (2016). YouTube vloggers' influence on consumer luxury brand perceptions and intentions. *Journal of Business Research*, *69*(12), 5753–5760

Lee, Y. G., Lopez, P. A., & Kelley, H. H. (2022). Associations between financial stressors and financial behaviors: Does race/ethnicity matter?. *Journal of Financial Counseling and Planning*, *33*(3), 358–375.

Lempers, J. D., Clark-Lempers, D., & Simons, R. L. (1989). Economic hardship, parenting, and distress in adolescence. *Child Development*, 60(1), 25–39.

Lepore, S. J., & Revenson, T. A. (2014). Resilience and posttraumatic growth: Recovery, resistance, and reconfiguration. In L. G. Calhoun & R. G. Tedeschi (Eds.), *Handbook of posttraumatic growth* (pp. 24–46). Routledge.

Lewis, A. (Ed.). (2018). *The Cambridge handbook of psychology and economic behavior*. Cambridge University Press.

Lim, S. S., & Bone, M. (2022). Optimism, debt accumulation, and business growth. *Journal of Behavioral and Experimental Economics*, *97*, 101828.

Linley, P. A., & Joseph, S. (2004). Toward a theoretical foundation for positive psychology in practice. In P. A. Linley & S. Joseph (Eds.), *Positive psychology in practice* (pp. 713–731). John Wiley & Sons.

Linley, P. A., Joseph, S., Harrington, S., & Wood, A. M. (2006). Positive psychology: Past, present, and (possible) future. *The Journal of Positive Psychology*, *1*(1), 3–16.

Lomas, T., Hefferon, K., & Ivtzan, I. (2014). *Applied positive psychology*. Sage.

Lomas, T., Pawelski, J. O., & VanderWeele, T. J. (2024). A flexible map of flourishing: The dynamics and drivers of flourishing, well-being, health, and happiness. *International Journal of Wellbeing*, *13*(4), 3665, 1–38.

Lomas, T., Waters, L., Williams, P., Oades, L. G., & Kern, M. L. (2021). Third wave positive psychology: Broadening towards complexity. *The Journal of Positive Psychology*, *16*(5), 660–674.

Lone, U. M., & Bhat, S. A. (2024). Impact of financial literacy on financial well-being: A mediational role of financial self-efficacy. *Journal of Financial Services Marketing*, 29(1), 122–137.

Lusardi, A. (2012). *Numeracy, financial literacy, and financial decision-making* (No. w17821). National Bureau of Economic Research.

Lusardi, A. (1999). Behavioral dimensions of retirement economics. In H. Aaron (Ed.), *Information, expectations, and savings*. Brookings Institution/Russell Sage Foundation.

Lusardi, A., & Mitchell, O. S. (2014). The economic importance of financial literacy: Theory and evidence. *Journal of Economic Literature*, *52*(1), 5–44.

Lusardi, A., & Mitchell, O. S. (2007). Baby boomer retirement security: The roles of planning, financial literacy, and housing wealth. *Journal of Monetary Economics*, *54*(1), 205–224.

Lusardi, A., Mitchell, O. S., & Curto, V. (2010). Financial literacy among the young. *Journal of Consumer Affairs*, *44*(2), 358–380.

Lusardi, A., Schneider, D. J., & Tufano, P. (2011). Financially fragile households: Evidence and implications. *National Bureau of Economic Research*, report no. w17072.

Lusardi, A., & Tufano, P. (2015). Debt literacy, financial experiences, and overindebtedness. *Journal of Pension Economics & Finance*, *14*(4), 332–368.

Lyall, C., Bruce, A., Tait, J., & Meagher, L. (2011). *Interdisciplinary research journeys*. Bloomsbury Academic.

Lyons, A. C., Grable, J. E., & Joo, S. H. (2018). A cross-country analysis of population aging and financial security. *The Journal of the Economics of Ageing*, *12*, 96–117.

Lyubomirsky, S., & Lepper, H. S. (1999). A measure of subjective happiness: Preliminary reliability and construct validation. *Social Indicators Research*, *46*, 137–155.

Lyubomirsky, S., Sheldon, K. M., & Schkade, D. (2005). Pursuing happiness: The architecture of sustainable change. *Review of General Psychology*, *9*, 111–131.

MacLeod, A. K., Coates, E., & Hetherton, J. (2008). Increasing well-being through teaching goal-setting and planning skills: Results of a brief intervention. *Journal of Happiness Studies*, *9*(2), 185–196.

Maddux, J. E. (2005). Stopping the "madness": Positive psychology and the deconstruction of the illness ideology and the DSM. In C. R. Snyder & S. J. Lopez (Eds.), *Handbook of positive psychology* (pp. 13–25). Oxford University Press.

Magli, A. S., Sabri, M. F., Abdul Rahim, H., & Othman, M. A. (2021). Influence of financial behavior, financial stress and locus of control on financial well-being among B40 households in Selangor during the pandemic. *Academic Research in Business and Social Sciences*, *11*(12), 468–486.

Magwegwe, F. M., MacDonald, M. M., Lim, H., & Heckman, S. J. (2023). Determinants of financial worry. *Journal of Consumer Affairs*, *57*(1), 171–221.

Mahdzan, N. S., Sukor, M. E. A., Zainudin, R., Zainir, F., & Wan Ahmad, W. M. (2023). A comparison of financial well-being and its antecedents across different employment categories in Malaysia. *Gadjah Mada International Journal of Business*, *25*(3), 255–277.

Mahendru, M., Sharma, G. D., Pereira, V., Gupta, M., & Mundi, H. S. (2022). Is it all about money honey? Analyzing and mapping financial well-being research and identifying future research agenda. *Journal of Business Research*, *150*, 417–436.

Malik, F., & Ishaq, M. I. (2023). Impact of minimalist practices on consumer happiness and financial well-being. *Journal of Retailing and Consumer Services*, *73*, 103333.

Malvaso, A., & Kang, W. (2022). The relationship between areas of life satisfaction, personality, and overall life satisfaction: An integrated account. *Frontiers in Psychology*, *13*, 894610.

Mani, A., Mullainathan, S., Shafir, E., & Zhao, J. (2013). Poverty impedes cognitive function. *Science*, *341*(6149), 976–980.

Mankiw, N. G. (2021). *Principles of economics* (8th ed.). Cengage Learning.

Marbin, D., Gutwinski, S., Schreiter, S., & Heinz, A. (2022). Perspectives in poverty and mental health. *Frontiers in Public Health*, *10*, 975482.

Margolin, G., & Gordis, E. B. (2004). Children's exposure to violence in the family and community. *Current Directions in Psychological Science*, 13(4), 152–155.

Martin, F. (2014). *Money*. Vintage.

Marx, K. (1887). *Capital*. Humboldt.

Mathew, V., & Sanjeev, M. A. (2024). Financial well-being and its psychological determinants—an emerging country perspective. *FIIB Business Review*, *13*(1), 42–55.

Matz, S. C., & Gladstone, J. J. (2020). Nice guys finish last: When and why agreeableness is associated with economic hardship. *Journal of Personality and Social Psychology*, *118*(3), 545–561

Mayo, C. O., Pham, H., Patallo, B., Joos, C. M., & Wadsworth, M. E. (2022). Coping with poverty-related stress: A narrative review. *Developmental Review*, *64*, 101024.

McAdams, D. P., & Olson, B. D. (2010). Personality development: Continuity and change over the life course. *Annual Review of Psychology*, *61*(1), 517–542.

McChesney, F. S. (2013). Behavioral economics: Old wine in irrelevant new bottles? *Supreme Court Economic Review*, *21*(1), 43–76.

McDonald, P. (2020). The male marriage premium: Selection, productivity, or mployer preferences? *Journal of Marriage and Family*, *82*(5), 1553–1570.
McEwen, B. S., & Stellar, E. (1993). Stress and the individual: Mechanisms leading to disease. *Archives of Internal Medicine*, *153*(18), 2093–2101.
Meadows, D. H. (2008). *Thinking in systems: A primer*. Chelsea Green Publishing.
Menezes, K., de Oliveira-Smith, P., & Woodworth, A. V. (Eds.). (2021). *Programming for health and well-being in architecture*. Routledge.
Milanovic, B. (2016). *Global inequality*. Harvard University Press.
Minichiello, V., & Coulson, I. (Eds.). (2012). *Contemporary issues in gerontology: Promoting positive ageing*. Routledge.
Mirza, H. S., & Warwick, R. (2024). Race and ethnic inequalities. *Oxford Open Economics*, 3, i365–i452.
Mishkin, F.-S. (2016). *The economics of money, banking, and financial markets* (11th ed.). Pearson.
Mistry, R. S., Vandewater, E. A., Huston, A. C., & McLoyd, V. C. (2002). Economic well-being and children's social adjustment: The role of family process in an ethnically diverse low-income sample. *Child Development*, *73*(3), 935–951.
Mitchell, O. S., & Lusardi, A. (2011). Financial literacy around the world: An overview. *Journal of Pension Economics and Finance*, *10*(4), 497–508.
Mohanty, M. S. (2012). Effects of positive attitude and optimism on wage and employment: A double selection approach. *The Journal of Socio-Economics*, *41*(3), 304–316.
Monat, J. P., & Gannon, T. F. (2015). What is systems thinking? A review of selected literature plus recommendations. *American Journal of Systems Science*, *4*(1), 11–26.
Monks, H., Mandzufas, J., & Cross, D. (2022). *The impact of poverty on the developing child: A narrative review*. Life Course Centre Working Paper, 6.
Morduch, J., & Schneider, R. (2017). *The financial diaries: How American families cope in a world of uncertainty*. Princeton University Press.
Morgan, E. V. (1969). *A history of money*. Penguin Books.
Mosley, P., & Lenton, P. (2012). *Financial exclusion and the poverty trap*. Routledge.
Mpaata, E., Koske, N., & Saina, E. (2023). Does self-control moderate financial literacy and savings behavior relationship? A case of micro and small enterprise owners. *Current Psychology*, *42*(12), 10063–10076.
Mueller, G., & Plug, E. (2006). Estimating the effect of personality on male and female earnings. *Ilr Review*, *60*(1), 3–22.
Munyon, T. P., Carnes, A. M., Lyons, L. M., & Zettler, I. (2020). All about the money? Exploring antecedents and consequences for a brief measure of perceived financial security. *Journal of Occupational Health Psychology*, *25*(3), 159.
Murendo, C., & Mutsonziwa, K. (2017). Financial literacy and savings decisions by adult financial consumers in Zimbabwe. *International Journal of Consumer Studies*, *41*(1), 95–103.
Nagypal, E., & Tobacman, J. (2019). *Credit characteristics, credit engagement tools, and financial well-being* (Office of Research Report No. 2019-07). Consumer Financial Protection Bureau.
Nakazato, N., Schimmack, U., & Oishi, S. (2011). Effect of changes in living conditions on well-being: A prospective top–down bottom–up model. *Social Indicators Research*, *100*, 115–135.
Nandru, P., Chendragiri, M., & Velayutham, A. (2021). Examining the influence of financial inclusion on financial well-being of marginalized street vendors: An empirical evidence from India. *International Journal of Social Economics*, *48*(8), 1139–1158.

Netemeyer, R.G., Warmath, D., Fernandes, D., & Lynch Jr., J.G. (2018). How am I doing? Perceived financial well-being, its potential antecedents, and its relation to overall well-being. *Journal of Consumer Research*, *45*(1), 68–89.
Ng, Y. K. (2003). From preference to happiness: Towards a more complete welfare economics. *Social Choice and Welfare*, 20(2), 307–350.
Nosratabadi, S., Fathi, Z., & Shoul, A. (2019). Investigating the effect of the framework of individual and group acts on the stock trading activities in Tehran stock exchange. *Cogent Business & Management*, 6(1), 1699310.
Nower, L., & Blaszczynski, A. (2006). Impulsivity and pathological gambling: A descriptive model. *International Gambling Studies*, 6(1), 61–75.
O'Connor, R. C., & Kirtley, O. J. (2017). Socioeconomic disadvantage and suicidal behaviour: psychological factors. In *Socioeconomic disadvantage and suicidal behaviour* (pp. 94–125). Samaritans.
Oehler, A., & Wedlich, F. (2018). The relationship of extraversion and neuroticism with risk attitude, risk perception, and return expectations. *Journal of Neuroscience, Psychology, and Economics*, *11*(2), 63–92.
ONS. (2023). *Personal well-being in the UK: April 2022 to March 2023*. Office of National Statistics UK.
ONS. (2022). *Household total wealth in Great Britain: April 2020 to March 2022*. Office of National Statistics UK, Statistical Bulletin.
ONS. (2018). *Measuring wealth on an individual level*. Office of National Statistics UK, statistical bulletin.
Oliver, M. L., & Shapiro, T. M. (2006). *Black wealth, white wealth*. Routledge.
OECD. (2024). *How's life? Wellbeing and resilience in times of crisis*. Organization for Economic Cooperation Development Publishing.
OECD. (2017). *How's life? Measuring well-being*. Organization for Economic Cooperation Development Publishing.
Ostroy, J. M., & Starr, R. M. (1990). The transactions role of money. In B. M. Friedman & F. H. Hahn (Eds.), *Handbook of monetary economics* (Vol. 1, pp. 3–62). Elsevier.
Otero-Lopez, J. M., & Villardefrancos, E. (2013). Five-factor model personality traits, materialism, and excessive buying: A mediational analysis. *Personality and Individual Differences*, *54*(6), 767–772.
Ozer, G., Kutbay, A., & Ozbek, V. (2017). The effects of budgeting, saving and compulsive buying on financial well-being of individuals. *Route Educational and Social Science Journal*, 4, 175–185.
Pahl, J. (1995). His money, her money: Recent research on financial organisation in marriage. *Journal of Economic Psychology*, *16*(3), 361–376.
Pak, T. Y., Fan, L., & Chatterjee, S. (2023). Financial socialization and financial well-being in early adulthood: The mediating role of financial capability. *Family Relations*, *73*(3), 1664–1685.
Papp, L. M., Cummings, E. M., & Goeke-Morey, M. C. (2009). For richer, for poorer: Money as a topic of marital conflict in the home. *Family Relations*, *58*(1), 91–103.
Parkin, M. (2011). *Economics* (10th ed.). Pearson.
Parks, A. C., & Biswas-Diener, R. (2013). Positive interventions: Past, present and future. In T. B. Kashdan & J. V. Ciarrochi (Eds.), *Mindfulness, acceptance, and positive psychology* (pp. 140–165). New Harbinger.
Parvathy, V. K., & Kumar, J. (2022). Financial capability and financial wellbeing of women in community-based organizations: Mediating role of decision-making ability. *Managerial Finance*, *48*(9/10), 1513–1529.
Pashler, H., & Wagenmakers, E. J. (2012). Editors' introduction to the special section on replicability in psychological science: A crisis of confidence? *Perspectives on Psychological Science*, 7(6), 528–530.

Pavot, W. (2018). The cornerstone of research on subjective well-being: Valid assessment methodology. In E. Diener, S. Oishi, & L. Tay (Eds.), *Handbook of well-being* (pp. 83–93). DEF Publishers.

Pavot, W., & Diener, E. (2004). Findings on subjective well-being: applications to public policy, clinical interventions, and education. In P. A. Lineley & S. Joseph (Eds.), *Positive psychology in practice* (pp. 679–692). Wiley.

Pawelski, J. O. (2016). Defining the 'positive' in positive psychology: Part II. A normative analysis. *The Journal of Positive Psychology*, 11(4), 357–365.

Pearlin, L. I., Menaghan, E. G., Lieberman, M. A., & Mullan, J. T. (1981). The stress process. *Journal of Health and Social Behavior*, 337–356.

Pedrotti, J. T., Lopez, S. J., McDermott, R. C., & Snyder, C. R. (2024). *Positive psychology*. Sage.

Peetz, J., & Robson, J. (2021). Living gig to gig and paycheque to paycheque. Centre for Economic Policy Research.

Peirce, R. S., Frone, M. R., Russell, M., & Cooper, M. L. (1994). Relationship of financial strain and psychosocial resources to alcohol use and abuse: The mediating role of negative affect and drinking motives. *Journal of Health and Social Behavior*, 35(4), 291–308.

Pereira, M. C., & Coelho, F. (2020). Regulatory focus, money attitudes and financial literacy: Evidence from Portuguese young adults. *Journal of Family and Economic Issues*, *41*(4), 615–625.

Perry, V. G., & Morris, M. D. (2005). Who is in control? The role of self-perception, knowledge, and income in explaining consumer financial behavior. *Journal of Consumer Affairs*, *39*(2), 299–313.

Pfeffer, F. T., & Schoeni, R. F. (2016). How wealth inequality shapes our future. *Russell Sage Foundation Journal of the Social Sciences*, 2(6), 2–22.

Philippas, N. D., & Avdoulas, C. (2022). Financial literacy and financial well-being among generation-Z university students: Evidence from greece. In J. O. Wilson, G. A. Panos, & C. Adcock (Eds.), *Financial literacy and responsible finance in the FinTech Era* (pp. 64–85). Routledge.

Piketty, T. (2014). *Capital in the twenty-first century*. Harvard University Press.

Pilch, I., & Gornik-Durose, M. E. (2017). Grandiose and vulnerable narcissism, materialism, money attitudes, and consumption preferences. *The Journal of Psychology*, *151*(2), 185–206.

Pillai, K. G., & Nair, S. R. (2021). The effect of social comparison orientation on luxury purchase intentions. *Journal of Business Research*, *134*, 89–100.

.Pincus, J. D. (2023). Well-being as need fulfilment: Implications for theory, methods, and practice. *Integrative Psychological and Behavioral Science*, 58(4), 1541–1579.

Pindyck, R. S., & Rubinfeld, D. L. (2018). *Microeconomics* (9th ed.). Pearson.

Pollard, E., & Lee, P. (2003). Child well-being: A systematic review of the literature. *Social Indicators Research*, *61*(1), 9–78.

Ponchio, M. C., Cordeiro, R. A., & Gonçalves, V. N. (2019). Personal factors as antecedents of perceived financial well-being: Evidence from Brazil. *International Journal of Bank Marketing*, *37*(4), 1004–1024.

Prawitz, A. D., Garman, E. T., Sorhaindo, B., O'Neill, B., Kim, J., & Drentea, P. (2006). InCharge financial distress/financial well-being scale: Development, administration, and score interpretation. *Journal of Financial Counseling and Planning*, *17*(1), 34–50.

Price, R. H., Choi, J. N., & Vinokur, A. D. (2002). Links in the chain of adversity following job loss: How financial strain and loss of personal control lead to depression, impaired functioning, and poor health. *Journal of Occupational Health Psychology*, 7(4), 302.

Prochaska, J. O., & Prochaska, J. M. (2019). Transtheoretical model. In J. M. Rippe (Ed.), *Lifestyle medicine* (3rd ed., pp. 219–228). CRC Press.

Prochaska, J. O., Redding, C. A., & Evers, K. E. (2015). The transtheoretical model and stages of change. In K. Glanz, B. K. Rimer, & L. Viswanath (Eds.), *Health behavior* (pp. 125–148). Wiley.

Puce, M. (2019). Challenges of applying behavioural economics: Critiques and limitations. *Journal of Behavioral Economics for Policy*, *3*(1), 41–48.

Quoquab, F., Mohammad, J., & Sukari, N. N. (2019). A multiple-item scale for measuring sustainable consumption behaviour construct: Development and psychometric evaluation. *Asia Pacific Journal of Marketing and Logistics*, *31*(4), 791–816.

Rafien, N. S. M., Awang, A. H., & Kamis, R. (2022). The effects of financial knowledge, financial attitude and locus of control on financial well-being among students in Malaysian public university: An empirical investigation. *Sciences*, *12*(12), 134–142.

Rai, K., Gupta, A., & Tyagi, A. (2021). Personality traits leads to investor's financial risk tolerance: A structural equation modelling approach. *Management and Labour Studies*, *46*(4), 422–437.

Rantakeisu, U., Starrin, B., & Hagquist, C. (1999). Financial hardship and shame: A tentative model to understand the social and health effects of unemployment. *The British Journal of Social Work*, *29*(6), 877–901.

Ranyard, R. (Ed.). (2018). *Economic psychology*. Wiley.

Ranyard, R., & de Mello Ferreira, V. R. (2018). Introduction to economic psychology: The science of economic mental life and behavior. In R. Ranyard (Ed.), *Economic psychology* (pp. 3–18). Wiley.

Rashid, S., Bilal, S., Hussain, S., & Shah, S. A. (2022). Impact of financial inclusion on financial well-being: Moderating effect of orientation towards finance. *Journal of Economic Impact*, *4*(2), 124–133.

Rashid, T., & Seligman, M. E. P. (2018). *Positive psychotherapy*. Oxford University Press.

Rath, T., & Harter, J. K. (2010). *Wellbeing: The five essential elements*. Simon and Schuster.

Reniers, R. L., Beavan, A., Keogan, L., Furneaux, A., Mayhew, S., & Wood, S. J. (2017). Is it all in the reward? Peers influence risk-taking behaviour in young adulthood. *British Journal of Psychology*, *108*(2), 276–295.

Reyers, M. (2019). Financial capability and emergency savings among South Africans living above and below the poverty line. *International Journal of Consumer Studies*, *43*(4), 335–347.

Ricardo, D. (1817). *On the principles of political economy and taxation*. John Murray.

Riitsalu, L., Atkinson, A., & Pello, R. (2023). The bottlenecks in making sense of financial well-being. *International Journal of Social Economics*, *50*(10), 1402–1422.

Riitsalu, L., & van Raaij, W. F. (2022). Current and future financial well-being in 16 countries. *Journal of International Marketing*, *30*(3), 35–56.

Riitsalu, L., & van Raaij, W. F. (2020). Self-control, future time perspective and savings–The keys to perceived financial well-being. *Technical Report*, 1–35.

Roberts, B. W., Luo, J., Briley, D. A., Chow, P. I., Su, R., & Hill, P. L. (2017). A systematic review of personality trait change through intervention. *Psychological Bulletin*, *143*(2), 117.

Roffey, S. (2011). *Positive relationships*. Springer.

Roka, D. (2020). The effect of human development on happiness: A comparative study of UN member states. *International Journal of Science and Business*, *4*(4), 61–78.

Rosso, V. F., Munoz-Pascual, L., & Galende, J. (2024). Do managers need to worry about employees' financial stress? A review of two decades of research. *Human Resource Management Review*, *34*(3), 101030.

Rothwell, D. W., Khan, M. N., & Cherney, K. (2018). Building financial knowledge is not enough: Financial self-efficacy as a mediator in the financial capability of low-income families. In J. Birkenmaier, M. Sherraden, J. J. Frey, C. Callahan, & A. M. Santiago (Eds.), *Financial capability and asset building with diverse populations* (pp. 12–32). Routledge.

Roy-Chaudhuri, H., Mazumdar, S., & Ghoshal, A. (2011). Conspicuous consumption orientation: Conceptualisation, scale development and validation. *Journal of Consumer Behaviour*, *10*(4), 216–224.

Rusk, R. D., & Waters, L. E. (2013). Tracing the size, reach, impact, and breadth of positive psychology. *The Journal of Positive Psychology*, *8*(3), 207–221.

Ryff, C.D. (2014). The structure of psychological well-being revisited. Psychotherapy and Psychosomatics, 83 (1), 10–28.

Sabri, M., Wijekoon, R., & Rahim, H. (2020). The influence of money attitude, financial practices, self-efficacy and emotion coping on employees' financial well-being. *Management Science Letters*, *10*(4), 889–900.

Saez, E., & Zucman, G. (2016). Wealth inequality in the United States since 1913: Evidence from capitalized income tax data. *The Quarterly Journal of Economics*, *131*(2), 519–578.

Salignac, F., Hamilton, M., Noone, J., Marjolin, A., & Muir, K. (2020). Conceptualizing financial wellbeing: An ecological life-course approach. *Journal of Happiness Studies*, *21*, 1581–1602.

Salignac, F., Marjolin, A., Reeve, R., & Muir, K. (2019). Conceptualizing and measuring financial resilience: A multidimensional framework. *Social Indicators Research*, *145*, 17–38.

Samuelson, P. A., & Nordhaus, W. D. (2010). *Economics* (19th ed.). McGraw-Hill.

Santiago, C. D., Wadsworth, M. E., & Stump, J. (2011). Socioeconomic status, neighborhood disadvantage, and poverty-related stress: Prospective effects on psychological syndromes among diverse low-income families. *Journal of Economic Psychology*, *32*(2), 218–230.

Saunders, P. (2006). *Social class and stratification*. Routledge.

Schmalor, A., & Heine, S. J. (2022). The construct of subjective economic inequality. *Social Psychological and Personality Science*, *13*(1), 210–219.

Schulz, A. J., Mentz, G., Lachance, L., Johnson, J., Gaines, C., & Israel, B. A. (2012). Associations between socioeconomic status and allostatic load: Effects of neighbourhood poverty and tests of mediating pathways. *American Journal of Public Health*, *102*(9), 1706–1714.

Schultz, D. P., & Schultz, S. E. (2011). *A history of modern psychology*. Cengage Learning.

Segerstrom, S. C. (2007). Optimism and resources: Effects on each other and on health over 10 years. *Journal of Research in Personality*, *41*(4), 772–786.

Segerstrom, S. C., Carver, C. S., Scheier, M. F. (2017). Optimism. In M. Robinson & M. Eid (Eds.), *The happy mind*. Springer.

Seligman, M. E. P. (2012). *Flourish*. Free Press.

Seligman, M. E. P. (2006). *Learned optimism*. Vintage.

Seligman, M. E. P. (2005). Positive psychology, positive prevention, and positive therapy. In C. R. Snyder & S. J. Lopez (Eds.), *Handbook of positive psychology* (pp. 3–9). Oxford University Press.

Seligman, M. E. P. (1999). The president's address. *American Psychologist, 54*, 559–562.
Seligman, M. E. P., & Csikszentmihalyi, M. (2000). Positive psychology: An introduction. *American Psychologist, 55*, 5–14.
Seligman, M. E. P., Parks, A. C., & Steen, T. (2004). A balanced psychology and a full life. *Philosophical Transactions of the Royal Society of London. Series B: Biological Sciences, 359*(1449), 1379–1381.
Shah, A.K., Zhao, J., Mullainathan, S., & Shafir, E. (2018). Money in the mental lives of the poor. *Social Cognition, 36*(1), 4–19.
Shah, A. K., Mullainathan, S., & Shafir, E. (2012). Some consequences of having too little. *Science, 338*(6107), 682–685.
Shaw, B.A., Agahi, N., & Krause, N. (2011). Are changes in financial strain associated with changes in alcohol use and smoking among older adults?. *Journal of Studies on Alcohol and Drugs, 72*(6), 917–925.
She, L., Ma, L., Voon, M. L., & Lim, A. S. S. (2023). Excessive use of social networking sites and financial well-being among working millennials: A parallel-serial mediation model. *International Journal of Bank Marketing, 41*(1), 158–178.
Shebib, S. J., & Cupach, W. R. (2018). Financial conflict messages and marital satisfaction: The mediating role of financial communication satisfaction. *Psychology, 9*(1), 144–163.
Shim, S., Serido, J., Tang, C., & Card, N. (2015). Socialisation processes and pathways to healthy financial development for emerging young adults. *Journal of Applied Developmental Psychology, 38*, 29–38.
Shim, S., Xiao, J. J., Barber, B. L., & Lyons, A. C. (2009). Pathways to life success: A conceptual model of financial well-being for young adults. *Journal of Applied Developmental Psychology, 30*(6), 708–723.
Shrider, E. A., & Creamer, J. (2023). Poverty in the United States: 2022. *US Census Bureau, 12*.
Sidra, S. (2025). Investigation of the dimensions and measurement of compensatory consumption behavior at different scales. *IROCAMM-International Review of Communication and Marketing Mix, 8*(1), 106–128.
Silber, D., Hoffmann, A. O., & Belli, A. (2024). When "good enough" is not good enough: How maximizing benefits financial well-being. *Psychology & Marketing, 41*(2), 308–327.
Simon, H. A. (1976). From substantive to procedural rationality. In T. J. Kastelein, S. K. Kuipers, W. A. Nijenhuis, & R. G. Wagenaar (Eds.), *25 years of economic theory* (pp. 65–86). Springer.
Simon, H. A. (1960). *The new science of management decision*. Harper & Brothers.
Sin, N. L., & Lyubomirsky, S. (2009). Enhancing well-being and alleviating depressive symptoms with positive psychology interventions: A practice-friendly meta-analysis. *Journal of Clinical Psychology, 65*(5), 467–487.
Sirgy, M. J. (1998). Materialism and quality of life. *Social Indicators Research, 43*, 227–260.
Sirin, S. R. (2005). Socioeconomic status and academic achievement: A meta-analytic review of research. *Review of Educational Research, 75*(3), 417–453.
Sivertsen, B., Hysing, M., & Bøe, T. (2025). The association between financial strain, psychological distress and subsequent depression: Findings from a Norwegian national study. *BJPsych Open, 11*(6), e254.
Sloman, J., & Garratt, D. (2010). *Essentials of economics*. Pearson Education.
Smith, A. (2019). *Consumer behaviour and analytics*. Routledge.
Smith, A. (1776). *An inquiry into the nature and causes of the wealth of nations*. Clarendon Press.
Snyder, C. R. (1994). *The psychology of hope*. Simon and Schuster.

Snyder, C. R., Cheavens, J. S., & Michael, S. T. (2005). Hope theory: History and elaborated model. In J. A. Eliott (Ed.), *Interdisciplinary perspectives on hope* (pp. 101–118). Nova.

Snyder, C. R., Lopez, S. J., Edwards, L. M., & Marques, S. C. (Eds.). (2020). *The Oxford handbook of positive psychology*. Oxford University Press.

Solomon, M. R. (2020). *Consumer behavior* (13th ed.). Pearson.

Song, C. L., Pan, D., Ayub, A., & Cai, B. (2023). The interplay between financial literacy, financial risk tolerance, and financial behaviour: The moderator effect of emotional intelligence. *Psychology Research and Behavior Management*, 16, 535–548.

Soria, K.M., Weiner, B., & Lu, E. C. (2014). Financial decisions among undergraduate students from low-income and working-class social class backgrounds. *Journal of Student Financial Aid*, *44*(1), 2.

Spilerman, S. (2000). Wealth and stratification processes. *Annual Review of Sociology*, *26*(1), 497–524.

Stajkovic, A. D., Greenwald, J. M., & Stajkovic, K. S. (2022). The money priming debate revisited: A review, meta-analysis, and extension to organizations. *Journal of Organizational Behavior*, *43*(6), 1078–1102.

Statista. (2024). *Financial wellbeing of people in Ireland survey 2024*. Statista Research Dept.

Stigler, G. J. (1961). The economics of information. *Journal of Political Economy*, *69*(3), 213–225.

Stiglitz, J. E., Sen, A., & Fitoussi, J. P. (2009). *The measurement of economic performance and social progress revisited* (Vol. 33). OFCE.

Stromback, C., Lind, T., Skagerlund, K., Västfjäll, D., & Tinghög, G. (2017). Does self-control predict financial behavior and financial well-being?. *Journal of Behavioral and Experimental Finance*, 14, 30–38.

Suls, J., Martin, R., & Wheeler, L. (2002). Social comparison: Why, with whom, and with what effect?. *Current Directions in Psychological Science*, *11*(5), 159–163.

Swain, R. B., & Floro, M. (2007). *Effect of microfinance on vulnerability, poverty and risk in low income households* (Working Paper 31). Department of Economics, Uppsala University.

Swanton, T. B., & Gainsbury, S. M. (2020). Debt stress partly explains the relationship between problem gambling and comorbid mental health problems. *Social Science & Medicine*, *265*, 113476.

Swarup, S. S., Padhi, B. K., Satapathy, P., Shabil, M., Bushi, G., Gandhi, A. P., Khatib, M. N., Gaidhane, S., Zahiruddin, Q. S., Rustagi, S., Barboza, J. J., & Sah, R. (2024). Cardiovascular consequences of financial stress: A systematic review and meta-analysis. *Current Problems in Cardiology*, *49*(2), 102153.

Sweet, E., Nandi, A., Adam, E. K., & McDade, T. W. (2013). The high price of debt: Household financial debt and its impact on mental and physical health. *Social Science & Medicine*, *91*, 94–100.

Szendrey, J., & Fiala, L. (2018). "I think I can get ahead!" Perceived economic mobility, income, and financial behaviors of young adults. *Journal of Financial Counseling and Planning*, *29*(2), 290–303.

Taft, M., Hosein, Z., Mehrizi, S., & Roshan, A. (2013). The relation between financial literacy, financial wellbeing and financial concerns. *International Journal of Business and Management*, *8*(11), 63–75.

Takeuchi, D. T., Williams, D. R., & Adair, R. K. (1991). Economic stress in the family and children's emotional and behavioral problems. *Journal of Marriage and the Family*, 53(4), 1031–1041.

Tamborini, C. R., Kim, C., & Sakamoto, A. (2015). Education and lifetime earnings in the United States. *Demography*, *52*(4), 1383–1407.

Tang, T. L. P. (1992). The meaning of money revisited. *Journal of Organizational Behavior*, 13(2), 197–202.

Tang, T. L. P. (1995). The development of a short money ethics scale: Attitudes toward money and pay satisfaction revisited. *Personality and Individual Differences*, *19*(6), 809–816.

Tang, T. L. P., & Chiu, R. K. (2003). Income, money ethic, pay satisfaction, commitment, and unethical behavior: Is the love of money the root of evil for Hong Kong employees?. *Journal of Business Ethics*, *46*, 13–30.

Tarde, G. (1902). *La Psychologie Economique* (2 vols). Alcan.

Tay, L., Zyphur, M., & Batz, C. L. (2018). Income and subjective well-being: Review, synthesis, and future research. In E. Diener, S. Oishi, & L. Tay (Eds.), *Handbook of well-being*. DEF Publishers.

Taylor, M. G., Carr, D. C., Carpenter, R., & Quesnel-Vallee, A. (2024). Work and income instability and retirement financial wellbeing for women and men. *Journal of Women & Aging*, *36*(3), 197–209.

Thaler, R. H. (2015). *Misbehaving*. WW Norton & Company.

Thaler, R. H. (1993). *Advances in behavioral finance*. Russell Sage Foundation.

Thaler, R. H., & Shefrin, H. M. (1981). An economic theory of self-control. *Journal of Political Economy*, *89*(2), 392–406.

Thaler, R. H., & Sunstein, C. R. (2008). *Nudge*. Yale University Press.

Therborn, G. (2013). *The killing fields of inequality*. Polity.

Trani, J. F., Moodley, J., Maw, M. T. T., & Babulal, G. M. (2022). Association of multidimensional poverty with dementia in adults aged 50 years or older in South Africa. *JAMA Network Open*, *5*(3), e224160.

Tsurumi, T., Yamaguchi, R., Kagohashi, K., & Managi, S. (2021). Material and relational consumption to improve subjective well-being: Evidence from rural and urban Vietnam. *Journal of Cleaner Production*, *310*, 127499.

Tversky, A., & Kahneman, D. (1974). Judgment under uncertainty: Heuristics and biases. *Science*, *185*(4157), 1124–1131.

UNDP. (2024). *Human development report 2023–24: Breaking the gridlock: Reimagining cooperation in a polarized world*. United Nations Development Programme.

Uppal, S., & LaRochelle-Cote, S. (2015). *Changes in wealth across the income distribution, 1999 to 2012*. Statistics Canada.

Unguren, E., Onur, N., Demirel, H.,& Tekin, O. A. (2024). The effects of job stress on burnout and turnover intention: The moderating effects of job security and financial dependency. *Behavioral Sciences*, *14*(4), 322.

DHH. (2024). *HHS pverty guidelines for 2024*. Federal Register Notice, USA, Department of Health and Human Services.

Vaccarino, V., & Bremner, J. D. (2024). Stress and cardiovascular disease: An update. *Nature Reviews Cardiology*, *21*(9), 603–616.

VanderWeele, T. J., & Lomas, T. (2023). Terminology and the well-being literature. *Affective Science*, *4*(1), 36–40.

Van Raaij, W.F. (2016). *Understanding consumer financial behavior*. Palgrave Macmillan.

Van Rooij, M. C., Lusardi, A., & Alessie, R. J. (2012). Financial literacy, retirement planning and household wealth. *The Economic Journal*, *122*(560), 449–478.

Van Rooij, M. C, Lusardi, A., & Alessie, R .J. (2011). Financial literacy and stock market participation. Journal of Financial Economics, *101*(2), 449–472.

Van Tran, D., Nguyen, T., & Nguyen, D. M. (2023). Understanding how upward social comparison stimulates impulse buying on image-sharing social commerce platforms: A moderated mediation model of benign envy and self-esteem. *Current Psychology*, *42*(22), 18777–18792.

Van Zyl, L. E., Gaffaney, J., van der Vaart, L., Dik, B. J., & Donaldson, S. I. (2024). The critiques and criticisms of positive psychology: A systematic review. *The Journal of Positive Psychology*, *19*(2), 206–235.
Vasicek, B., Zigraiová, D., Hoeberichts, M., Vermeulen, R., Šmídková, K., & de Haan, J. (2017). Leading indicators of financial stress: New evidence. *Journal of Financial Stability*, *28*, 240–257.
Veblen, T. (1899). *The theory of the leisure class*. Macmillan.
Velandia-Morales, A., Rodríguez-Bailón, R., & Martínez, R. (2022). Economic inequality increases the preference for status consumption. *Frontiers in Psychology*, *12*, 809101.
Verplanken, B., & Herabadi, A. (2001). Individual differences in impulse buying tendency: Feeling and no thinking. *European Journal of Personality*, *15*(Suppl 1), S71–S83.
Vinokur, A. D., Price, R. H., & Caplan, R. D. (1996). Hard times and hurtful partners: how financial strain affects depression and relationship satisfaction of unemployed persons and their spouses. *Journal of Personality and Social Psychology*, *71*(1), 166–179.
Vlaev, I., & Elliott, A. (2014). Financial well-being components. *Social Indicators Research*, *118*, 1103–1123.
Vogler, C., & Pahl, J. (1994). Money, power and inequality within marriage. *The Sociological Review*, *42*(2), 263–288.
Vohs, K. D. (2015). Money priming can change people's thoughts, feelings, motivations, and behaviors: An update on 10 years of experiments. *Journal of Experimental Psychology*, *144*(4), e86–e93.
Von Stumm, S., O'Creevy, M. F., & Furnham, A. (2013a). Financial capability and money beliefs. *Journal of Applied Social Psychology*, *43*(8), 1453–1467.
Von Stumm, S., O'Creevy, M. F., & Furnham, A. (2013b). Financial capability, money attitudes and socioeconomic status: Risks for experiencing adverse financial events. *Personality and Individual Differences*, *54*, 344–349.
Wadsworth, M. E., Raviv, T., Santiago, C. D., & Etter, E. M. (2011). Testing the adaptation to poverty-related stress model: Predicting psychopathology symptoms in families facing economic hardship. *Journal of Clinical Child & Adolescent Psychology*, *40*(4), 646–657.
Walker, I., & Zhu, Y. (2003). Education, earnings and productivity: recent UK evidence. *Labour Market Trends*, *111*(3), 145–152.
Warren, M. A., Donaldson, S. I., & Luthans, F. (2017). Taking positive psychology to the workplace: Positive organizational psychology, positive organizational behavior, and positive organizational scholarship. In M. A. Warren & S. I. Donaldson (Eds.), *Scientific advances in positive psychology* (pp. 195–227). Praeger.
Warwas, I., Podgórniak-Krzykacz, A., Wiktorowicz, J., & Górniak, J. (2022). Demographic and generational determinants of Poles' participation in the sharing economy: Findings from a survey data analysis. *PLoS One*, *17*(6), e0265341.
Watson, D., Clark, L. A., & Tellegen, A. (1988). Development and validation of brief measures of positive and negative affect: The PANAS scales. *Journal of Personality and Social Psychology*, 54(6), 1063–1070.
Weatherford, J. (1998). *The history of money*. Crown Business.
Wei, C., Dang, J., Liu, L., Li, C., Tan, X., & Gu, Z. (2023). Economic inequality breeds corrupt behaviour. *British Journal of Social Psychology*, *62*(2), 949–971.
Whillans, A. V., Dunn, E. W., Sandstrom, G. M., Dickerson, S. S., & Madden, K. M. (2016). Is spending money on others good for your heart?. *Health Psychology*, *35*(6), 574–583.

Wilkinson, N., & Klaes, M. (2018). *An introduction to behavioral economics*. Bloomsbury.
Wilkinson, R. G., & Pickett, K. E. (2010). *The spirit level: why equality is better for everyone*. Penguin Books.
World Bank. (2022). *Poverty and shared prosperity: Correcting course*. World Bank.
Xiao, J. J., Huang, J., Goyal, K., & Kumar, S. (2022). Financial capability: A systematic conceptual review, extension and synthesis. *International Journal of Bank Marketing*, *40*(7), 1680–1717.
Xiao, J. J., & Kim, K. T. (2022). The able worry more? Debt delinquency, financial capability, and financial stress. *Journal of Family and Economic Issues*, *43*(1), 138–152.
Xiao, J. J., Kim, K. T., & Lee, S. (2024). Consumer financial capability and financial wellbeing; multi-year analyses. *Applied Research in Quality of Life*, *19*(2), 547–580.
Xiao, J. J., & O'Neill, B. (2018). Propensity to plan, financial capability, and financial satisfaction. *International Journal of Consumer Studies*, *42*(5), 501–512.
Xin, S., Yin-Fah, B. C., & Dada, M. (2020). Comparison of people's financial wellbeing between China and Malaysia. *Electronic Journal of Business & Management*, *5*(1), 14–22.
Yoshino, N., & Morgan, P. J. (2020). *Financial literacy and fintech adoption in Japan* (ADBI Working Paper No. 1095). Asian Development Bank Institute.
Yu, Y., & Williams, D. R. (1999). Socioeconomic status and mental health. In R. T. Serpe (Ed.), *Handbook of the sociology of mental health* (pp. 151–166). Springer.
Yulfa, R., & Herawati, T. (2017). The influence of social support and financial management toward family well-being in early marriage. *Journal of Family Sciences*, *2*(2), 45–57.
Zagorski, K., Evans, M. D., Kelley, J., & Piotrowska, K. (2014). Does national income inequality affect individuals' quality of life in Europe? Inequality, happiness, finances, and health. *Social Indicators Research*, *117*, 1089–1110.
Zhang, J. W., Howell, R. T., & Howell, C. J. (2016). Living in wealthy neighborhoods increases material desires and maladaptive consumption. *Journal of Consumer Culture*, *16*(1), 297–316.
Zhang, Y., & Chatterjee, S. (2023). Financial well-being in the United States: The roles of financial literacy and financial stress. *Sustainability*, *15*(5), 4505.
Zizzo, D. J. (2010). Experimenter demand effects in economic experiments. *Experimental Economics*, *13*, 75–98.
Zyphur, M. J., Li, W. D., Zhang, Z., Arvey, R. D., & Barsky, A. P. (2015). Income, personality, and subjective financial well-being: The role of gender in their genetic and environmental relationships. *Frontiers in Psychology*, *6*, 1493.

Glossary

Allostatic load: The cumulative physiological wear and tear on the body that results from chronic stress.

Barter system: A system of exchange in which goods or services are traded for other goods or services.

Behavioural Economics: A scientific field rooted in Economics that incorporates psychological insights.

Big Five/Five Factor Model: A widely used model of personality that describes five broad traits: openness, conscientiousness, extraversion, agreeableness and neuroticism.

Compensatory consumption: Consumption undertaken to offset negative feelings.

Conspicuous/Status-oriented consumption: The purchase or display of goods and services for the purpose of signalling wealth, status or social standing to others.

Consumption within the sharing economy: Consumption that takes place through systems of shared access, temporary use, exchange or peer-to-peer provision rather than through outright ownership.

Economic Psychology: An interdisciplinary field integrating Psychology and Economics to examine how psychological factors influence economic behaviour and how economic conditions influence people's lives.

Economic wellbeing: A form of wellbeing that applies to units such as organisations, communities and nations.

Ethical consumption: Consumption guided by moral concerns about how goods and services are produced, traded and consumed.

Eudaimonic wellbeing: The functioning-well aspect of wellbeing.

Financial disorders: Persistent and maladaptive patterns of thought, emotion or behaviour in relation to money that interfere with healthy financial functioning.

Financial flourishing: A positive state of financial wellbeing.

Financial inclusion: Access to and use of financial products and services.

Financial literacy: Knowledge and understanding of financial concepts, products and practices.

Financial Planning: A professional and applied field concerned with helping individuals and households achieve financial goals through structured planning and decision support.

Financial Psychology: A sub-domain of Economic Psychology that applies psychological theory and method to personal finance.

Financial resilience: The capacity to cope with, recover from and adapt to financial shocks, setbacks or uncertainty.

Financial wellbeing: A state in which a person or household can meet financial obligations, feel secure about the future and make choices that enable them to meet needs and enjoy life.

Flourishing: A high state of wellbeing.

Gig workers: Workers who earn income through short-term, task-based, freelance, platform-based or other non-standard forms of employment.

Green consumption/sustainable consumption/environmentally friendly consumption: Consumption choices intended to reduce environmental harm and support ecological sustainability.

Happiness Economics: A research area examining the relationship between money and happiness.

Hedonic wellbeing: The feeling-good aspect of wellbeing.

Homo economicus: A classical economic model of the person as rational, self-interested, utility-maximising and fully informed economic actor.

Impulse buying: Spontaneous, immediate purchasing with little prior planning or deliberation.

Income: The monetary compensation received by an individual or household from sources such as employment, business activity, investments or state support.

Indebtedness: The state of owing money through liabilities such as loans, credit card balances, mortgages or other financial obligations.

Locus of control: A psychological construct referring to whether people perceive outcomes as primarily contingent on their own actions (internal locus of control) or on external forces such as luck, fate or powerful others (external locus of control).

Macroeconomics: The branch of Economics that examines aggregate economic activity, including inflation, national income, growth and government policy.

Materialism: A value orientation that gives priority to wealth and possessions.

Microeconomics: The branch of Economics concerned with the actions and interactions of individuals, households and firms in markets.

Money priming: A psychological process whereby exposure to money-related cues influences cognition, emotion and behaviour.

Overall wellbeing: A broad concept referring to how well a person is doing across life as a whole.

Positive Economic Psychology: An interdisciplinary field integrating Positive Psychology and Economic Psychology.

Positive Psychology: A branch of Psychology focused on the scientific study and practical promotion of wellbeing.

Poverty: A socioeconomic condition marked by insufficient financial and material resources to secure a basic standard of living.

Prosocial behaviour: Behaviour intended to benefit others.

Relative income: An individual's or household's income considered in comparison with that of a reference group.

Relative wealth: An individual's or household's wealth considered in comparison with that of a reference group.

Resilience: The ability to withstand challenges, recover from difficulty and adapt positively.

Risk aversion: A tendency to prefer certainty over uncertainty and to avoid choices that involve the possibility of loss.

Risk tolerance: A person's willingness to accept uncertainty, variability or the possibility of loss in financial decision-making.

Self-control/self-regulation: The capacity to regulate impulses, emotions, attention and behaviour in line with longer-term goals or standards.

Self-efficacy: A person's belief in their ability to carry out actions successfully and achieve desired outcomes.

Social comparison: The process through which people evaluate themselves by comparing their circumstances, abilities or status with those of others.

Socialisation: The lifelong process through which individuals learn values, norms, knowledge and behavioural patterns from family, peers, institutions and culture.

Socioeconomic status (SES): A person's or group's social and economic standing within society, commonly assessed through income, education and occupation.

Subjective wellbeing: A broad term commonly used in academic literature to refer to happiness.

Time orientation: A person's habitual orientation towards the past, present or future when thinking, deciding and acting.

Utility: A term used in Economics which pertains to the satisfaction or benefit derived from a good, service or economic choice or action.

Wealth: The total value of an individual's or household's financial and non-financial assets after liabilities are taken into account.

Wellbeing: A broad, multidimensional concept concerned with living well.

Index